From Your Friends At **The MAILBOX® Magazine**

Teacher Tips
Preschool/Kindergarten

D0474032

Editor In Chief
Marge Michel

Product Director
Kathy Wolf

Editors
Ada Goren, Angie Kutzer, Mackie Rhodes

Copy Editors
Laurel Robinson, Debbie Shoffner

Artists
Jennifer Tipton Bennett, Cathy Spangler Bruce, Pam Crane, Teresa Davidson, Susan Hodnett, Sheila Krill, Rebecca Saunders, Barry Slate, Donna K. Teal

Typographers
Scott Lyons, Lynette Maxwell

Cover Artist
Jennifer Tipton Bennett

Teacher Tips
Preschool/Kindergarten

About This Book

We've compiled hundreds of never-before-published ideas sent from our subscribers to *The Mailbox®* magazine—The Idea Magazine For Teachers®. These ideas were submitted to The Education Center, Inc., from preschool and kindergarten teachers all over the United States and Canada.

The ideas in this resource are arranged so that you can refer to a topic quickly and choose just the idea you need. In each section, you'll find creative ways to teach a skill, management tips, or activities to fill in a few extra minutes of the teaching day. We've chosen a range of adaptable ideas, to help you work with younger preschoolers or more advanced kindergartners. Look in several sections for ideas to suit your individual needs.

Just turn these pages to find timesaving, teacher-tested tips to help make your teaching easier and more creative!

Table Of Contents

My Teacher's In The Mail!

Imagine the excitement each of your students will experience when he receives this "sneak-a-peek-at-the-teacher" greeting in the mail! For each child, duplicate a photograph of yourself on the right side of a sheet of paper. Add some color to the copied picture, if desired. Then trim and fold the paper in greeting-card fashion so that your picture becomes the card front. Inside the card, write a personalized message to welcome the child to school and to tell him about back-to-school events. Then mail a card to each child prior to the scheduled events. Look! It's my teacher in the mail!

Kay Dawson—Gr. K
B. C. Charles Elementary
Newport News, VA

Dear Abbey,
  I'm glad you are in my class. I hope to see you on "Meet Your Teacher" Night next Tuesday from 6:30–8:00 P.M.

Love,
Ms. Dawson
Room 10
B. C. Charles Elementary

All Aboard

Toot! Toot! A back-to-school train theme will be just the ticket to get your class chugging along on the right track. To begin, duplicate one of the train tickets and the engineer's cap on page 145 on blue construction paper for each child; then cut out each ticket and cap. Mail a ticket and a welcome letter to each child, mentioning that he should bring his ticket to class on the first day of school. To prepare each engineer cap, cut the slits as indicated on the pattern; then—starting from the back of the cutout—thread a one-inch wide, black construction-paper strip through the slits.

On the first day of class, collect each child's ticket; then invite him to wear an engineer's cap. Adjust the headband to fit the child's head and staple the ends together. For an additional touch, have each child wear a bandanna, too. Encourage youngsters to wear their engineer attire throughout the day as they engage in train-related activities—such as singing train songs, reading train books, and switching centers on a train-whistle signal. If desired, videotape the outfitted youngsters; then conclude your theme activities with a showing of the video. All aboard for a great school year!

Marjorie Eisenwine, South St. Marys Street Elementary, St. Marys, PA

"Get To Know Me" Bags

Invite youngsters to bag some information about themselves to share with classmates on the first day of school. Prepare a welcome letter instructing each child to decorate the enclosed bag, then fill it with things that will help the class get to know her—such as an item representing her favorite color, a photo of her pet, or a wrapper from her favorite candy. Mail the letter along with a paper bag labeled "Get To Know Me" and bearing the child's name. On the first day of school, invite each child to remove and tell about the contents of her bag. With this idea, making first-day friends is in the bag!

Cynthia Corey—Gr. K
Heritage Christian School
Canton, OH

Eye-Appealing Apple Name Cards

Use these cute 3-D name cards for your back-to-school and first-day-of-school decorations. To make a name card, duplicate the apple pattern on page 146 on red construction paper. Cut out each pattern; then fold the cutout along the dotted line between the apples. Attach a brown construction-paper stem to the top of the apple. Write the child's name on both sides of the stem. Then attach a green construction-paper leaf to each side of the apple. Fold the bottom strips of the apple toward each other; then glue the strips together to create a stand for the name card.

Karen Eiben—Three-Year-Olds
The Kids' Place
LaSalle, IL

Parent Database

For a quick and easy reference, compile your own parent database. Simply prepare a form requesting information about each parent's occupation, hobbies, interests, and skills. Send a copy of the form home with each child. When students return the completed forms to school, file them in an accessible location. Then, when studying themes or planning for special projects, check your database to determine if any of your students' parents are potential sources of information or help during those activities.

Carmen Rufa—Gr. K, Samaritan Children's Center, Troy, NY

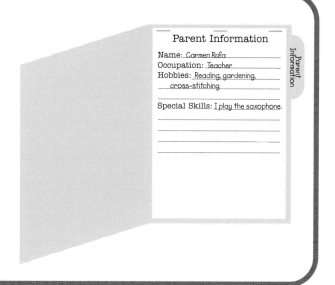

Parent Information

Name: Carmen Rufa
Occupation: Teacher
Hobbies: Reading, gardening, cross-stitching

Special Skills: I play the saxophone.

Take A Bus Tour

Invite youngsters and their parents to take a bus tour as part of your back-to-school events! Arrange to have a school bus or center van available during your meet-your-teacher activities. Then encourage your bus riders and their parents to take a tour of the bus. This brief tour will help youngsters become familiar with the inside of a bus and may help alleviate the anxiety that accompanies those first-day, bus-rider jitters.

Adapted from an idea by Peggy Klipstine—Gr. K, Early Childhood Center Denmark, Denmark, WI

Thomas Bennett
Bus Number 274
123 Park Lane

No-Worry Nametags

Curb that first-week anxiety and nervousness associated with riding the bus with these no-worry nametags. For each child, program a bus-shaped nametag with his name, his bus number, and the address of his destination. Laminate each nametag for durability; then punch a hole in the top of the nametag and add a length of yarn to create a necklace. Have each child put on his nametag prior to boarding the bus. What a reassuring feeling these nametags will give students, parents, and even the bus driver!

Amy Scott—Gr. K
St. Augustine School
Napoleon, OH

All About The Teacher

Give youngsters and their parents the opportunity to get to know you better with a book about yourself. Include photographs of yourself as a child, your family, your house, your pet, and yourself engaged in hobbies and interests. Write a brief statement about the pictures on each page to tell a story about yourself. Title the book "All About [your name]." Invite a different child to take the book home each week to share with his parents.

Bonnie Blanck—Gr. K
J. F. Dumont
Cincinnati, OH

My dog's name is Sam. He can roll over, fetch a stick, and bark really loud!

Parent Picture Perker-Uppers

When youngsters show signs of missing their parents during those first few days of school, this idea may provide the anxiety relief they need. During your back-to-school events, take a picture of each child's parents. Display the pictures at a child's eye level. Then, during the school day, if a child needs perking up or a gentle reminder that he will see his parents soon, guide him to his parent's picture and speak some reassuring words to him. Later in the school year, remove the pictures and have students use them to create parent gifts for a special occasion.

Connie A. Barry—Preschool Handicapped, Betsy Ross School, Mahwah, NJ

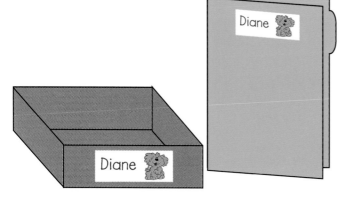

Simple Symbol System

Make name recognition simple when you use this symbol system. Using clip-art pictures, select a symbol that begins with the first letter of each child's name—such as an apple for Adam or jelly for Jessica. (Choose a different symbol for each child whose name begins with the same letter.) Make several copies of each symbol. Glue one copy of the symbol on a name card for each child; then attach the other copies near his name on his cubby, folders, journals, and other property assigned to that child. Encourage independence in each child by having him find his name on items and locations around the room, using the symbol as a cue.

Diane Golden—Four-Year-Olds
Roselle, NJ

Classmate Memory

This memory game will help youngsters learn their classmates' names and faces twice as fast! To prepare, take a photograph of each student; then order double prints when you have the film developed. After your double prints are returned, mount each picture on a separate tagboard card. Laminate the cards for durability. Then place all the cards facedown. To play, have a child turn over two cards, then name the child appearing on each of the cards. If the cards are a match, the player keeps them. If the cards do not match, the child returns them to their facedown position and another child takes a turn. Continue play until all the matches have been found.

Gina Mello—Three- and Four-Year-Olds
South Winneshiek Elementary
Ossian, IA

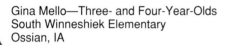

Wheel Of Friends

Students will be spinning to get to know one another with this special wheel. To make the wheel, cut out two identical, large poster-board circles. Evenly space and glue a separate picture of each child 1/2" from the edge of one of the circles. Cut out a photo-sized opening 1/2" from the edge of the other circle cutout; then position that circle on top of the first circle, covering all the student photos except the one beneath the cutout. Loosely attach the two circles together with a paper brad so that the top circle—or wheel—will spin freely. To use, have a youngster spin the wheel, then identify the student whose photo appears in the opening. Later in the school year, you might have students spin the wheel to pick partners or to determine the order of turn-taking in an activity. Or use the wheel to divide the class into small groups or to pick class helpers. With imagination and a flair for fun, there are dozens of ways to use this wheel of friends!

Kyle Welby—Gr. K
Epstein Hebrew Academy
St. Louis, MO

Who Do You See?

Here's a book that will help youngsters learn each other's names as well as engage them in predictive storytelling. To begin, take a picture of each child in your class; then have a volunteer take your picture and a picture of the entire class, including yourself. Program a sheet of white copy paper with text and blanks as shown. Duplicate the programmed sheet on construction paper for each child. Mount each child's picture on a separate page; then write her name on the blank lines of her page. Mount your photo on a sheet of construction paper programmed only at the bottom with "[Your name, your name], who do you see?" Mount the class picture on a sheet of construction paper programmed at the top with "I see everyone looking at me!" Stack the student pages between your page and the class page; then use metal rings to bind the pages together between two construction-paper covers. Write "Who Do You See?" on the front cover.

Read the book aloud with youngsters during group or storytime; then put it in your reading center for youngsters to enjoy. For variety—and to keep students interested in the book—periodically change the sequence of the student pages.

Jodi Laakso—Gr. K, Tower Hill School, Randolph, MA

Put Your Best Foot Forward

Invite little ones to start off the school year on their best foot with these goal-oriented footprints. Help each child trace his bare foot onto a sheet of construction paper; then have him cut out his footprint. Write his name and dictated goal for the year on his cutout. For example, a child may want to learn how to recite the alphabet, write his name, or assemble jigsaw puzzles. Display the footprints with the title "Put Your Best Foot Forward" as a reminder to youngsters to work toward their goals.

Cynthia Corey—Gr. K
Heritage Christian School
Canton, OH

Autographed Art

Your young artists will take pride in being able to autograph their own master-pieces by using these readily available name cards. To prepare, take a picture of each child; then glue each child's picture onto a tagboard card labeled with his name. Laminate the name cards for dura-bility. Punch a hole in the upper left corner of each card; then bind the cards together with a metal ring. Place the cards in your art center. Then encourage each child to copy his name onto his work, using his name card as a guide.

Lori F. Hartley—Three-, Four-, And Five-Year-Olds
George Hildebrand Family Resource Program
Morganton, NC

VIP Privileges

Reserve some special privileges for each child to enjoy during his assigned VIP—Very Important Person—week and watch his self-esteem grow! At the beginning of the year, assign each child a week to be the class VIP. On the first day of a child's assigned week, have him bring in some of his favorite photos of himself. Invite him to decorate a poster on which to display the pictures. Throughout the week give him special privileges—such as bringing or selecting a book for storytime, sitting in a special chair, and being a special helper. If he desires, allow the child to invite his parents to class for a day—and even to help them discuss their occupations or special skills with the class. At the end of a child's VIP week, present him with a special certifi-cate and invite him to select a prize from a special box.

Jodi Laakso—Gr. K
Tower Hill School
Randolph, MA

A "Class-y" Dress

Little ones will love the compliments their "hand-i-work" receives when you wear this student-decorated dress to school. In advance, purchase a solid-colored cotton dress. Then, before beginning your project, place a large piece of cardboard inside the dress to prevent paint leak-throughs. Using fabric paint, randomly write each student's name on the dress; then invite each child in turn to make a fabric-paint handprint beside his name. After the paint dries, take the dress home to be laundered according to label directions. Each time you wear the dress, notice how youngsters glow over the compliments you get on your "class-y" dress.

Kimberley Berringer—Gr. K
Dillard Street Elementary
Apopka, FL

Ms. Parette is our nurse.

She has a thermometer.

The nurse lets me hold a

bear when she puts a

bandage on my boo-boo.

Meet Your Neighbors

Take some time at the beginning of the school year to introduce youngsters to their school neighbors. Tell students they will go on a trip to meet some important people in their school neighborhood. Then invite them to board an imaginary bus or train to begin their trip around the school campus. Along the way, make stops to introduce the children to people whom they need to know—such as the principal or director, the nurse, or the cafeteria workers. Take a photograph of each person introduced to the students. After the class returns to the classroom, mount each photo on a separate sheet of chart paper; then ask youngsters to tell some things about each person. Write their responses on the appropriate chart. Display the charts with the title "Our School Neighbors." During the next few weeks, add student dictation to the charts as youngsters learn more about each helper. It's nice to know your neighbors!

Diane Parette—Gr. K
Durham Elementary
Durham, NY

Hands-On Learning For Parents!

Try this alternative to lecturing parents at Open House on the hows and whys of learning centers. Invite parents to play and explore in the centers, so they can discover the benefits on their own! With each activity, provide instructions along with a listing of skills practiced during that specific activity. Be sure to bring the parents together after center time to review what was learned. For added fun, take instant photos of parents at play and have them on display the next day for your students to see! You're never too old to learn!

Jodi Laakso—Gr. K
Tower Hill School
Randolph, MA

Open House Scavenger Hunt

Have students help you prepare a scavenger hunt for parents to complete during Open House. Write the children's list of items, areas, and displays that they would like to share with their parents in a checklist format. If desired, include simple pictures that illustrate each listing. Reproduce a classroom supply of checklists. At Open House, explain the hunt to parents and encourage them to ask their children for help. Students will be so excited, they won't let their parents rest until they've completed this quest!

Diane Parette—Gr. K
Durham Elementary
Durham, NY

As an addition to the scavenger hunt idea, ask parents to turn in their lists before they leave your classroom. The next day attach a "Good Work" sticker to each list, write a note thanking the parent for attending Open House, and send the list home with the child.

Bernadette Hoyer—Pre-K
Howard B. Brunner School
Scotch Plains, NJ

CHECK OUT OUR ROOM!

- puppets ☐
- attendance board ☐
- my cubby ☐
- calendar ☐
- writing center ☐
- classroom pet ☐
- 3 pieces of my best work ☐

Child's Name _____

Adult's Name _____

The Gang's All Here

Get ready for Open House with this "person-able" display. Trace around each child's body on a length of bulletin-board paper. Provide crayons, markers, yarn, buttons, and other various art materials for her to use in decorating her body outline. When the decorating is done, cut out each outline. On the day of Open House, place each child's figure in her chair. Tape the cutout hands to the table or desk and the cutout legs to the seat so that the figure is sitting in an upright position. Parents will be surprised to see their little ones sitting so quietly when they arrive!

Amy Pierce—Pre-K, Pierce Private Day School, Irving, TX

An "A-peel-ing" Open House

Start a new tradition with this tasty Open House treat. Purchase a long length of rain gutter and line it with foil. During Open House, invite youngsters and their parents to build a super-sized banana split in the foil-lined gutter. After Open House presentations, scoop servings into disposable bowls and invite parents and children to dig in!

Deborah Well—Gr. K, B. R. Ryall YMCA, Glen Ellyn, IL

Perky Pumpkins

This pumpkin patch will welcome your parents to Open House with faces all aglow! To make these free-standing pumpkins, duplicate a class supply of the pumpkin pattern from page 146 on orange construction paper; then cut them out. On one side of each cutout write "Welcome!" and on the other side, write a child's name. Fold the bases on the dotted lines and staple them together. Add a stem, leaf, and vine using scraps of green paper.

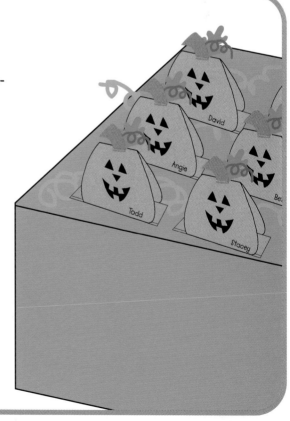

To create the pumpkin patch, cover a tabletop or countertop with green bulletin-board paper. Arrange the cutouts on the paper and scatter green, plastic grass between them. Add pieces of green curling ribbon to resemble vines. Parents will be proud to see their "li'l punkins" represented in this festive display!

Karen Eiben—Three-Year-Olds
The Kids' Place
LaSalle, IL

A Birthday Book

Youngsters will delight in these birthday books made especially for them! Draw a birthday-cake pattern on a sheet of paper. Duplicate a classroom supply of the pattern for each child; then cut them out. Or if desired, use sheets from cake-shaped notepads. On a student's birthday, distribute a cake shape to each child and have her draw a picture for the birthday child. At the top of the cake help her write "From:" and her name. Instruct the birthday child to decorate his page to serve as the cover of the book. Title the book "Happy Birthday To [child's name]!" Stack the pages behind the cover, punch holes along the left side, and bind the book with yarn. What a beautiful birthday keepsake!

Carolyn Bryant—Pre-K
First Baptist Church Powder Springs
Powder Springs, GA

Party Pendants

Here's an inexpensive and time-saving tip for making birthdays special. Cut apart the shapes on birthday-themed borders to use as pendants. Punch a hole at the top of each pendant; then add a length of colored yarn. If desired, label each pendant with a different child's name and age. It's a "border-ific" birthday!

Janice Lagard—Four-Year-Olds
Discovery Years
Hamburg, NJ

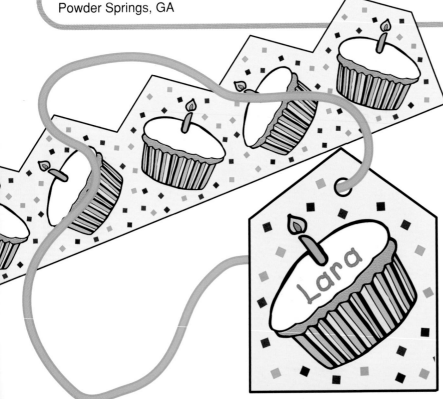

Birthdays Past

Invite children to celebrate birthdays past *and* present with this birthday timeline. In advance, make a classroom supply of large cake cutouts from bulletin-board paper with enough room to display a picture from each birthday year. For example, if you teach four-year-olds who are turning five, you'll need space on the cake for five pictures.

Invite the birthday child to bring a picture from each of his birthdays to share with the group. Mount these pictures with tape on a cake cutout labeled with his name; then take an instant photo of the child to display at the end of the timeline. My, how we've grown!

Tracey J. Quezada—Gr. K
Presentation Of Mary Academy
Hudson, NH

Crafty Crowns

Use plastic, gallon-size water bottles for making these birthday crowns that won't tear. To make a crown, cut off the bottom of the bottle; then cut a four-inch band from the middle section. Cut points in the band along one side. Use a permanent marker to write the numeral for the birthday child's age on the crown; then decorate around the numeral with stickers. Your children will feel like royalty on their special days!

Eva Excaliber—Three- And Four-Year-Olds
Play And Learn Preschool At Temple Samuel
Miami, FL

Birthday Book Buddies

Celebrate birthdays with books! At the beginning of the year have children pick partners by drawing names from a hat. Before each child's birthday, provide her buddy with a book. Instruct the buddy to wrap the book in birthday paper and make a card for the birthday child. On the special day, have the buddy present the gift and card to the birthday child. Once the book is unwrapped, share it with the class. Good literature makes the day even more special!

Tracey J. Quezada—Gr. K
Presentation Of Mary Academy
Hudson, NH

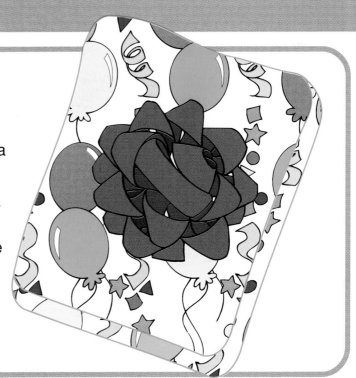

Party Wear

Help each child dress for the occasion with this birthday T-shirt. At the beginning of the school year, request that each child bring in a solid-colored T-shirt (a size larger than what she wears). Provide fabric paints and assist each student in creating a birthday cake on her shirt. When the paint is dry, label each shirt with the date of the child's birthday; then decorate the cake with the appropriate number of candles. Set all the shirts aside. The day before each child's birthday, send home her shirt so she can wear it to school the next day. Your little ones are sure to feel special wearing these terrific T-shirts!

Michele DeCroes—Gr. K
Cannella Elementary School
Tampa, FL

Happy Birthday To You

Make each child feel extraspecial by including them in this birthday big book. Use two large sheets of construction paper as covers. Write "Our Birthday Book" on the front cover. Bind the covers together with metal rings. On each child's birthday take a photo of him; then mount it on a piece of large construction paper. Under the photo write the child's thoughts about his birthday and any other information he wishes to share about himself. Have the child decorate his page; then bind it between the book covers. With each birthday, this book gets bigger and better.

Tracey J. Quezada—Gr. K
Presentation Of Mary Academy
Hudson, NH

lots of presents

my new swing set

Kyle's birthday is June 21. He likes birthdays because his relatives come to visit and bring neat stuff!

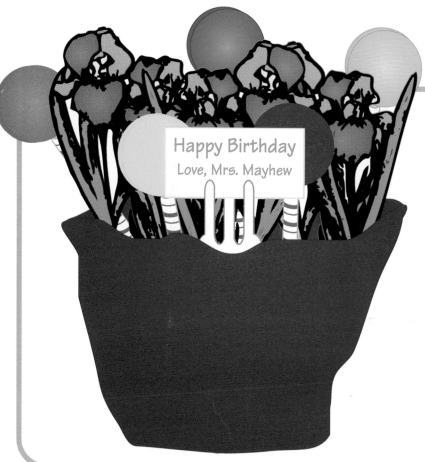

Happy Birthday
Love, Mrs. Mayhew

Birthday Bouquet

Present the birthday child with this unique gift at the end of his special day. Wrap the container of a small, flowering plant with metallic cellophane. Insert several straws—cut in different lengths—into the dirt; then insert a lollipop into each straw. Stick the handle of a plastic fork into the dirt at the front of the plant and add a card with a personal birthday greeting from you to the child. This colorful bouquet will help make the child's birthday at school a day to remember!

Space Identifiers

Do your youngsters have difficulty recognizing their names in order to find their cubbies or lockers? This idea may provide the solution. Take a snapshot of each child; then attach his picture and name card to his cubby or assigned space. Encourage each child to look for his picture *and* name to identify his space. In no time, students will be recognizing their names without relying on the picture prompts.

Kim Richman—Three-Year-Olds
The Learning Zone
Des Moines, IA

Classroom Memories

Is there a particular center, storage area, or furniture arrangement in your room that works really well? If so, then capture it on film and use the photos to set up your room for the new school year. Simply take pictures of the areas that you would like to duplicate in the following year. Then, when arranging your room, use the photos as a guide to help you place furniture, displays, storage containers, and other items. Looking at these pictures will bring back some great classroom memories!

Ellen S. Bruno—Gr. K–1 Special Education, Rio Rancho Elementary, Rio Rancho, NM

Now, Where's That Outlet Cover?

Have you misplaced that outlet cover again? Try this quick timesaving tip to eliminate the frustration of having to track down your outlet covers. Attach the loop side of a piece of Velcro® to the back of each outlet cover. Then attach the hook side of a piece of Velcro® to the wall beside each outlet. Each time you remove an outlet cover, simply attach it to the Velcro® on the wall beside the outlet. No more hide-and-seek games with outlet covers!

Karen Hattaway—Owner
Bright Beginnings Preschool, Inc.
Palmetto, FL

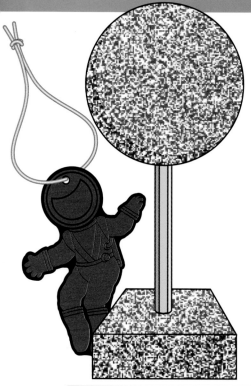

Planetary Center Sites

Your young astronauts will get a blast out of visiting learning centers marked by these planets. To prepare the planets, gather an unsharpened pencil, a Styrofoam® block, and a Styrofoam® ball for each center. Paint each set of items with a different color tempera paint. Assemble each planet by poking a hole in the block and ball with the pencil; then glue one end of the pencil in the hole in the block and the other end in the ball. Next, determine the desired number of students to use each center. Then duplicate that many copies of the astronaut pattern on page 153 on each color of construction paper corresponding with each planet color. Cut out and laminate the astronaut patterns; then punch a hole in the top of each cutout. Thread a length of yarn through the hole in each cutout and tie the yarn ends together to create a necklace. Place a different planet at each center; then, have each child select a necklace and go to the center marked by the same color planet.

Adapted from an idea by Lynn Cagney—Gr. K, Hunter's Green Elementary, Tampa, FL

In The Tube

Try this quick tip for storing plastic bags. Stuff several bags into a paper-towel tube. Then, when a bag is needed—such as for wet clothes or take-home items—simply pull a bag from the tube. Replenish the tube as needed. Easy!

Joan Banker—Four-Year-Olds, St. Mary's Child Development Center, Garner, NC

Shoe-Holder Organizer

Save steps and space when you use an over-the-door shoe holder to organize your materials. Purchase a shoe holder with clear vinyl pockets; then store a different kind of small item—such as rubber bands, pens, and scissors—in each separate pocket. If desired, label each pocket with its content's name. Hang the organizer over a door or on the wall for easy access. This idea is a "shoe-in" for step-saving simplicity!

Amy Pierce—Pre-K
Pierce Private Day school
Irving, TX

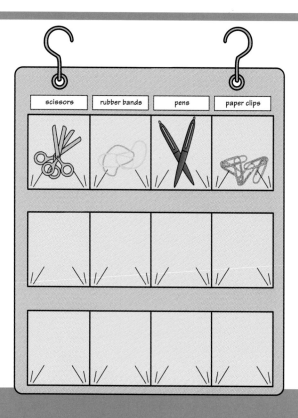

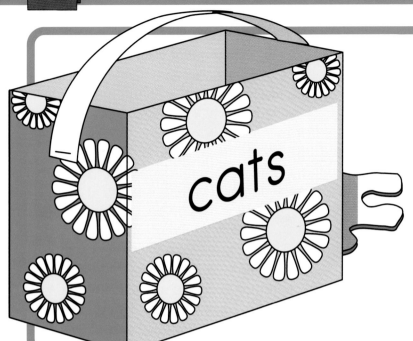

Floor-Puzzle Storage

Puzzled over how to store your floor puzzles? Try using detergent boxes. Cut off the lid of an empty laundry detergent box, leaving the handle intact. Cover the box with decorative Con-Tact® covering. Put a set of puzzle pieces in the box; then label the box with the puzzle name. Invite a youngster to tote the storage container to an open area of the floor, assemble the puzzle, and return the pieces to the box after he's finished.

Jackie Wright—Gr. K and Preschool
Summerhill Children's House
Enid, OK

Small-Item Storage

When play-dough canisters are no longer needed to store play dough, use them for small-item storage. Simply put a different type of small object—such as paper clips, wiggle eyes, or pushpins—in each clean canister; then label the canister with its contents, and put the lid on it. This storage tip is a snap!

Jennifer Peña—Pre-K, Normandy Village, Jacksonville, FL

Clear-View Storage Tubes

For a manipulative storage idea that's clearly unique, use plastic tennis-ball canisters. Remove the labels from empty, clear tennis-ball tubes; then put a different set of manipulative items into each tube—such as plastic animals, shells, buttons, or golf tees. Label each tube and store the containers in a tub or on a shelf. Encourage students to look at the contents in each see-through tube to pick out the manipulatives of their choice. It's clear—you're a sure winner with this idea!

Donna Mackie—Gr. K
Periwinkle Elementary
Albany, OR

Canned Borders

Ever wonder how to store your bulletin-board borders when they are not in use? Try canning them! Roll a border set so that it fits into a clean coffee can. Then glue a short length of the border around the can to serve as the label. Snap the lid on the can and presto! Your bulletin-board borders are safely stored!

Gina Mello—Three- And Four-Year-Olds
South Winneshiek Elementary
Ossian, IA

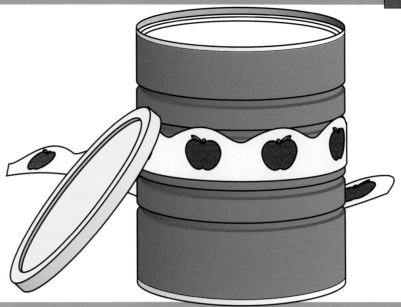

Snappy Storage

Clear plastic bakery containers with snap-on lids are perfect for storing lightweight classroom items. Put each type of object—such as feathers, pom-poms, or dried flowers—in a separate container. Place the lid on the container; then label the container with its contents. Store the containers on shelves—stacked or side by side. Youngsters can easily locate the items they need by looking at the contents in these see-through containers.

Alida Bockino—Gr. K, Lena Whitmore Elementary, Moscow, ID

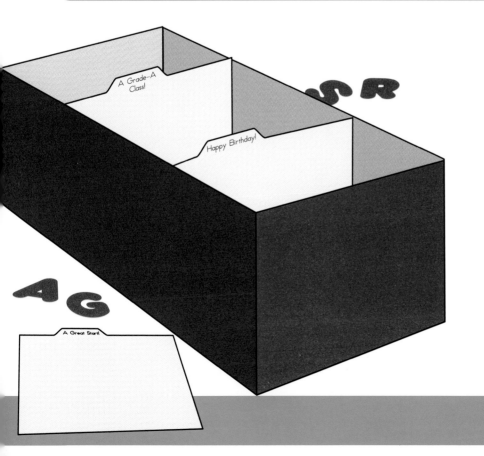

Easy-To-Find Bulletin-Board Titles

If you reuse your bulletin-board titles and letters, here's a simple tip to help keep them organized for easy retrieval. Cut tagboard or manila folders into file dividers sized to fit a shoebox, leaving a raised section at the top of each divider. Label each divider with a different bulletin-board title. Then, when the letters in that title are not in use, store them in the box behind the appropriate divider.

Amy Pierce—Pre-K
Pierce Private Day School
Irving, TX

Paper Collection Trays

Convert paper-box lids into nifty paper collection trays. To make a tray, cover the outside of a paper-box lid with decorative Con-Tact® covering. Turn the lid—or tray—upside down, and label it to indicate its use—such as "Letters To Parents," "Art," or even your own name for personal papers; then place the tray in an appropriate location in the classroom. Voila! It's a quick and easy organizer tray!

Joan Banker—Four-Year-Olds
St. Mary's Child Development Center
Garner, NC

Mini-Book Boxes

How many mini books can this mini-book box hold? Try this idea to find out! Clean and label a separate diaper-wipe box for each child. Throughout the school year, as each child completes a mini book, have him place it in his book box. Store the boxes in a convenient location, so students can reread the books often and share them with classmates. At the end of the year, have each child take his mini-book collection home for summer reading. To reuse the boxes for the next year, simply wipe the names off the boxes with cotton balls dampened with alcohol.

Alida Bockino—Gr. K
Lena Whitmore Elementary School
Moscow, ID

A-Tisket, A-Tasket, I Put It In The Basket

Avoid the hectic paper-shuffling that comes with the arrival of students each morning with this idea. Decorate a large straw or plastic basket with ribbons and artificial flowers. Label the basket with your name; then have youngsters put their notes from home, lunch-money envelopes, and other items not needing your immediate attention into the basket as they arrive each morning. Then, after the students are settled into other class activities, take some time to sort through and take care of the contents of the basket.

Amy Scott—Gr. K
St. Augustine School
Napoleon, OH

Pocket Song Chart

Help youngsters select circle-time songs to sing with this wordless pocket song chart. Hang an over-the-door shoe holder with clear vinyl pockets in your circle-time area. Place a different object in each pocket to represent the songs your students know. For instance, put a plastic pig in one pocket for "Old MacDonald," a toy bus for "Wheels On The Bus" in another pocket, and a felt happy face for "If You're Happy And You Know It" in yet another. During circle time, invite a child to select the object representing his song choice from the song chart; then have all the children sing that song. This pocket song chart is an ideal way to promote making choices.

Katherine Willett—Three- And Four-Year-Olds
Kaleidoscope Preschool
Hopkins, MN

See-Through Storage Packets

These clever storage packets allow you to store a variety of learning aids at your fingertips and make finding materials as easy as one, two, see! Purchase a supply of top-loading page protectors; then create packets by placing each of your flannelboard, learning center, and story-prop sets in a separate protector. Label each packet with the name of its contents and—if desired for future reference—the source from which it was taken. Store the packets in a three-ring binder, keeping related materials together. Then when you need specific items, simply browse through the book until you see what you need.

Katie Petersen—Four- And Five-Year-Olds
ADVOCAP/Headstart
Fond du Lac, WI

Bagged, Booked, And Boxed

Organize your theme-related books with this easy-to-use system. Place each book in a zippered plastic bag labeled with that book's theme or topic—such as bears or shapes. Record the book title and author under the same category in a notebook. Program a separate 3" x 5" card with each book's author and title; then file the cards by author's last name in a file box. Store the bagged books in a large box by category. To use, refer to the notebook to locate desired books by categories or check the file box to find books by their authors.

Cynthia Corey—Gr. K
Heritage Christian School
Canton, OH

Flannelboard Figures At Your Fingertips

Convert plain manila folders into storage packets for your flannelboard figures. To make a storage packet, staple the sides of a folder together along the edges, leaving the top edge open. Then insert the pieces of a flannelboard set into the top of the packet. If desired, store other related materials—such as a companion book or reproducible pages—in the packet also. Label the packet to indicate its contents; then file the packets in a file cabinet. When you need them, your flannelboard sets will be right at your fingertips.

Gina Mello—Three- And Four-Year-Olds
South Winneshiek Elementary
Ossian, IA

	Attendance	Permission Form Returned	Buying Lunch
Eva Davidson			
Ben Saunders			
Jackson Crane			
Samuel Crump			
Jahmal Amash			
Breyanna Mayworth			
Nicholas Bruck			
Keesha Walker			
Eli Loughran			
Mai Kotani			

Wipe-Off Enrollment Chart

Make this handy enrollment chart to serve as your attendance keeper and reminder board. On a sheet of chart paper, list each student's name on a separate line along the left side. Program the right side of the chart with several columns; then laminate the chart. Post the chart near your classroom door. To use the chart, label each column as desired with a wipe-off marker. For example, the columns might be labeled "Attendance," "Permission Form Returned," and "Buying Lunch." Then use the chart to keep track of the things listed by marking the appropriate columns by each child's name. At the end of the day, wipe the chart clean and program it for the next school day.

Diane Shatto—Three- And Four-Year-Olds
St. Elizabeth
Kansas City, MO

Easy-To-Use Attendance Chart

Keep daily attendance with this quick and easy idea. Write each child's name on a separate tagboard card; then laminate the cards for durability. Attach a piece of magnetic tape to the back of each name card. Place the cards on a file cabinet or magnetic board near the door. As each child enters the classroom, have him remove his name card, then place it in a pocket chart designated as the attendance chart. At a glance, you can check the remaining name cards to see which children are absent.

If desired, you might also use the chart to keep track of lunch purchases, returned permission forms, or items brought from home. Simply create two columns on the pocket chart. Then label each column with a picture card as desired—such as a lunchbox above one column and a lunchbox with an X over it above the other column. Have students place their name cards in the chart under the appropriate column. A quick scan of the names under each column will give you instant information.

Kristin Bates—Gr. K, Turner Elementary, West Chicago, IL

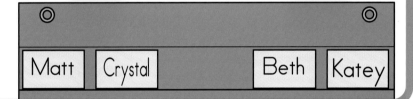

Durable Nametags

These nametags are so durable, they can be used for a number of purposes. For each child, cut a nametag from a plastic file folder or binder. Write the child's name on the nametag with a permanent marker; then punch a hole in the top of each nametag. To use, thread a length of yarn through the hole and tie the ends together to create a necklace. Or use the nametags to take attendance, to play name-recognition games, to line up students, or to group youngsters for center activities. These long-lasting nametags can be used in dozens of ways—your imagination is the limit!

Pam Szeliga—Pre-K
Riverview Elementary
Baltimore, MD

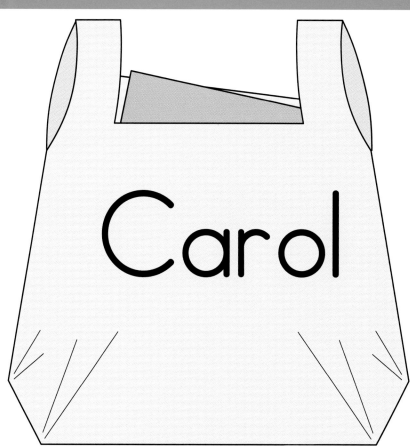

Bags To Go

Get youngsters ready to go with this earth-friendly tip! Store plastic grocery bags in a container near your youngsters' cubbies. Then, if a student forgets to bring his bookbag, simply pack his belongings in a plastic bag to send home. Or use a bag to send home items that do not fit into a child's bookbag. What a handy way to reuse those plastic bags.

Carol Babinsack—Three-, Four-, And Five-Year-Olds
Tuscarora Intermediate Unit II
McConnellsburg, PA

Lunchbox Messages

Here's an idea that will get parents' attention. Instead of sending home messages in a child's bookbag—where they may be forgotten or overlooked—try placing the notes in an envelope or zippered sandwich bag, then putting the envelope in her lunchbox or lunch bag. When the parent is ready to clean out the child's lunchbox and pack it for the next day, she'll be sure to find the message from school. With this system, notes will not go unnoticed, and you may even find that home-school correspondence occurs more smoothly and frequently!

Diane Shatto—Three- And Four-Year-Olds
St. Elizabeth
Kansas City, MO

Instant Name Labels

To help youngsters recognize their names, create these instant labels for them to use on their papers and artwork. Print each child's name repeatedly on a separate sheet of paper; then duplicate the name sheet as many times as desired. Cut apart the names so that you have one name on each strip. Place each child's name strips into a separate wall-chart pocket labeled with a symbol assigned to that child. Then encourage each child to glue one of his name strips onto each of his completed papers, works of art, or projects. In no time youngsters will be recognizing their names and, perhaps, even trying to write them!

Carol Babinsack—Three-, Four-, And Five-Year-Olds
Tuscarora Intermediate Unit II
McConnellsburg, PA

Easy Record-Keeping

Use this idea to keep an organized record of each youngster's progress. Print each child's name on a separate notebook divider; then place the dividers in a loose-leaf binder with several sheets of paper behind each of them. If desired, attach a pen to the notebook. To use, record the date and anecdotal notes about a child on a sheet of paper behind his divider. Add notes as frequently as desired, sequencing the notes by date. Then use the recorded information when writing out student progress reports and during parent conferences. This record-keeping notebook is an easy, effective way to document up-to-date progress for each student.

Lisa Cohen—Gr. K
Laurel Plains Elementary
New City, NY

Brag Books

Invite youngsters to help create these books that will give them plenty to brag about. To begin, give each child a three-ring binder to decorate as he desires. Throughout the year, date and attach student work—such as art papers, journal entries, letters, and photos—to hole-punched sheets of paper and insert them in the binder. Or use pocket dividers, sheet protectors, or photo album pages to hold the child's work. During the year, invite youngsters to share their brag books with classmates as well as with parents. As a bonus, each child's brag book will be a useful tool when holding parent conferences. At the end of the year, allow each child to take his brag book home as a keepsake of his school year.

Shari Gewanter—Three-, Four-, And Five-Year-Olds
Shady Lane School
Pittsburgh, PA

Timesaver Labels

Save time with these easy-to-use name labels. Use computer-generated plain or decorative labels with "From the desk of [Your Name]" to draw parents' attention to special papers and notes. You might create your labels on your own computer or purchase a special order of labels. Then just attach a label to any notes, forms, or other materials that you especially want parents to notice or read.

Marlene Kimmell—Gr. K
Graysville Elementary
Graysville, IN

From The Desk Of
Marlene Kimmell

Dear Parent,
Don't forget our field trip to the hospital tomorrow! Pack your child's lunch in a paper bag with a disposable drink container.
We'll leave school at 8:45 A.M.
Thanks!

Just Stamp It

Here's a simple way to date student work for filing. Keep a self-inking date stamp or a date stamp and stamp pad on hand. Set the date on the stamp each day. Then, as a student completes a piece of work that you plan to keep on file, just stamp it. It's that quick and easy!

Seema Gersten
Harkham Hillel Hebrew Academy
Beverly Hills, CA

Collage Collection Box

Prepare a collage collection box that will keep materials organized and separated as youngsters create their art masterpieces. Obtain a large compartmentalized box—such as the kind in which large quantities of crayons can be purchased. Or make cardboard dividers to fit inside a paper-box lid; then glue the dividers in place inside the box. Cover the outside of the box with decorative Con-Tact® covering. Then put a different type of collage material—such as feathers, buttons, fabric scraps, and colored pasta shapes—in each compartment. Encourage youngsters to combine a variety of the available items as they craft their unique creations.

Amy Pierce—Pre-K
Pierce Private Day School
Irving, TX

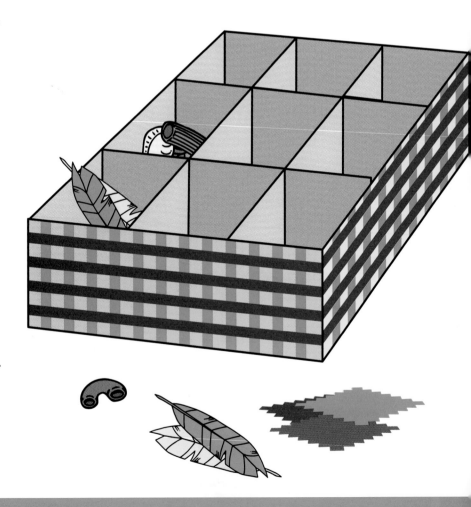

No-Mess Art Trays

Do away with the tedious task of cleaning up glitter, sand, or rice when you have students use these no-fuss, no-mess art trays. When a student is ready to put glitter or any other dry sprinkling material on his art paper or creation, have him place his work in a gift-box lid or bottom—a quick and easy art tray. Invite the child to sprinkle the glitter over his creation, then shake the excess off into the tray. Have the child remove his completed creation from the tray and set it aside. After using the trays, the glitter left in them can be returned to the original containers to be used again. These simple trays make cleaning up after sprinkling activities a breeze!

Alison Hynds—Gr. K
Shannon Forest Christian School
Greenville, SC

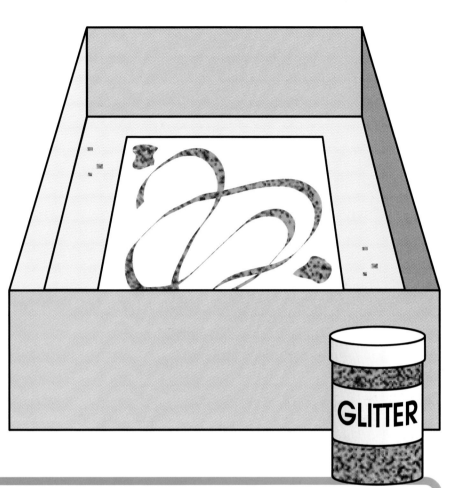

Recycled Dessert Cups

Instead of tossing emptied snack pudding and gelatin containers into the trash can, why not reuse them in your classroom? Wash each of the containers thoroughly; then use some of them in your art center as paint cups or for holding homemade play dough. Or have youngsters use some of the cups for sorting and counting small items. Place some in your sand or water table for students to use as scoops. Other uses might include using the cups as construction toys or in open-ended art projects.

Catherine Wyshyvanuk—Gr. K
St. Francis Xavier
Phoenix, AZ

Personal Art Supplies Organizer

Youngsters will be doing their part to keep the art center neat when they use their own personal art organizers. For each child, cover a clean, powdered baby-formula can with Con-Tact® covering; then label the can with the child's name. Place each child's crayons, scissors, glue, and other personal art supplies in the can. Shelve these personal organizers within easy reach of students. Encourage each student to retrieve her own organizer when using the art center; then have her return the organizer to the shelf when she is finished with the supplies. Youngsters will delight in taking responsibility for such a neat center!

Amy Pierce—Pre-K
Pierce Private Day School
Irving, TX

Easy-Grip Sponge-Painters

Get a handle on sponge-painting—by putting handles on your sponges! To do this, hot-glue an empty spool onto each sponge shape. Then engage youngsters in sponge-painting activities using the easy-grip, handled sponges. Students will find that these special sponges are easier to hold and are a much neater alternative to "handle-less" sponges!

Samita Arora—Pre-K
Richmond, IN

"I Wish I Could Take A Picture!"

How often have you spoken these words when a child has created a temporary masterpiece on the chalkboard or the Magna-Doodle®? Or even when he's constructed an extraordinary structure with the blocks or made an amazing discovery at the sensory table? Well, wish no more! Simply purchase several disposable cameras; then place each camera in a different, accessible location in the classroom. Whenever you want to capture a special moment on film, just grab the closest camera and snap away!

A Pool Of Ideas

These ideas on ways to use a plastic wading pool in your classroom year-round will make a big splash with youngsters! Try using the pool as a catch-all for messy art activities—such as glitter-sprinkling or splatter-painting—by having youngsters kneel beside the pool to make their creations. Or partially fill the pool with sand, rice, water, or another sensory material to allow students lots of free exploration. Or convert the pool into a cozy reading area by tossing in a few soft pillows and some interesting children's books. At other times, you might add different props to the pool to encourage imaginary play—such as plastic oars and life jackets or plastic spiders, sticks, yarn, and tape. Now, go ahead—dive in with some of your own unique uses for your pool!

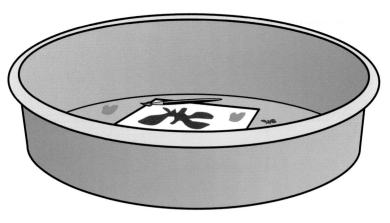

Marjorie A. Zimmer—Four- And Five-Year-Olds
Woods Chapel Early Childhood Education Center
Arlington, TX

Quick And Easy Borders

Personalize your displays with borders your children can make. Give each child a length of adding-machine tape. Have him use alphabet or seasonal sponges to sponge-paint his strip with his name, with random letters in different colors, or with a pattern. When the paint is dry, attach the strips together to frame classroom displays or bulletin boards. You'll have a child-centered classroom right down to the border!

Kathie Lipowski—Three-, Four-, And Five-Year-Olds
St. Mary's
Bedford, OH

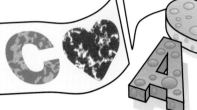
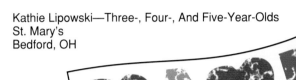

Puppets From The Kitchen?

Need more puppets for your dramatic play area? Try looking in the kitchen-supplies section of local department and discount stores for novelty pot holders. They are cute, durable, and inexpensive. Let the puppet parade begin!

Susan Brown—Gr. K
Southside Elementary
Tuscumbia, AL

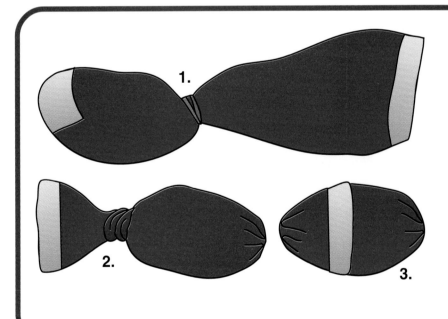

1.

2.

3.

Bargain Beanbags

Here's an inexpensive idea for making your own beanbags! Fill half of the foot of a brightly colored knee sock with dried beans. Gather the sock around the top of the beans and secure it with a rubber band. Turn the remainder of the sock inside out around the beans; then twist the sock and fold it over the beans again. This no-sew method is a real time-saver!

Lorrie Hartnett
Canyon Lake, TX

Critter Keeper

Invite children to observe creepy-crawlies through a clear, plastic cake container instead of an expensive observation tank. Punch small airholes in the top; then place the critter—along with some of its natural habitat—inside. If desired, keep a misting bottle handy to keep the environment moist. Use the container for short-term visits by neighborhood bugs or for the extended stay of caterpillars hatching into butterflies.

Cheryl B. Cicioni—Three-, Four-, And Five-Year-Olds
Kindernook Preschool
Lancaster, PA

Talking Trunk

Bring an elephant cutout to life with this puppet idea. Make a large elephant head and two ears from tagboard. Cut out the pieces; then attach the ears to the head. Cut a circle through the tagboard head where the elephant's trunk should connect. Add eyes with a marker or with construction paper. If desired, laminate the elephant; then cut away the plastic from the nose hole.

To use the puppet, slide a gray sock over your arm; then stick your arm through the nose hole. Ta da! A talking elephant!

Nancy Slotnick—Three- And Four-Year-Olds
The Kid's Space
Foxboro, MA

Dynamic Dice

Your children will enjoy rolling these big dice for various math activities. To make a die, stuff a sturdy, cube-shaped box with newspaper. Then wrap the box in solid-colored Con-Tact® covering. Use colored self-adhesive dots to program the die. For beginners, program two sides with one dot, two sides with two dots, and two sides with three dots. For more advanced children, program the die representing numbers one through six. Then roll out some fun!

Nikki Beller—Developmentally Delayed Preschool
Bucks County Intermediate Unit
Doylestown, PA

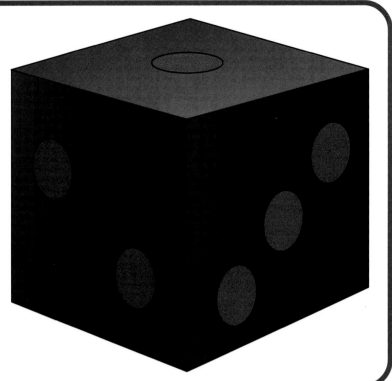

"Hand-y" Textures

Reinforce the concept that our hands help us determine how an object feels with this "hand-y" idea. Trace and cut out several hand shapes from cardboard. Cover each hand with a different medium—such as cotton, sandpaper, buttons, silk, or fake fur. Place the hands in a center and invite little ones to explore this touchy subject. This will be a favorite activity, hands down!

Tina Butterbaugh—Gr. K
His Majesty's Learning Center
Lexington, KY

Water Wonders

Use these fun water bottles to improve your students' visual tracking, to exercise gross-motor skills, or to create a soothing mood. Remove the label from clear, plastic, 16-ounce soda bottles. Put several colorful, water-resistant objects in each bottle—such as marbles, shells, buttons, or glitter. Fill the bottles with water, stopping about 1/2 inch from the top. If desired, add a few drops of food coloring; then screw the caps on tightly. For extra security, wrap the caps and seams with electrical tape. Invite your little ones to shake the bottles and watch the water wonders!

Marcia Buchanan—Preschool
Special People In Northeast, Inc.
Philadelphia, PA

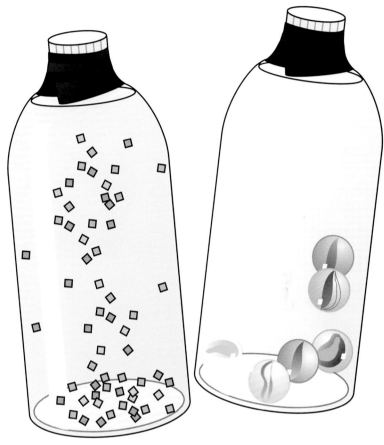

Picture Puppets

Here's an easy way to make stick puppets for your classroom. Cut pictures from old calendars and mount them onto tagboard. Laminate the pictures if desired; then glue a craft stick to the back of each one. These colorful puppets will add sparkle to your songs, stories, and units. When you're not using them, place them in the dramatic play area for students to manipulate. A puppet performance is sure to occur!

Tracey J. Quezada—Gr. K
Presentation Of Mary Academy
Hudson, NH

Border Magic

Take the expense out of buying borders by letting your children create them! Invite each child to decorate a colored sentence strip with a variety of art materials—such as markers, fabric scraps, sequins, and confetti. Trim a decorative edge on each strip if desired. Your bulletin boards and displays will welcome these unique *and* inexpensive borders!

Pam Szeliga—Pre-K
Riverview Elementary
Baltimore, MD

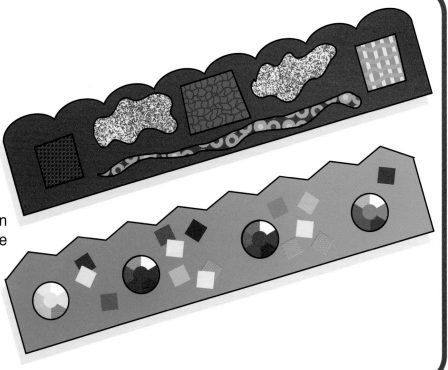

Indoor Snowballs

Is the weather outside too frightful? Stay inside and play with these nonmelting snowballs instead. To make a snowball, cut a five-inch band from a leg of white panty hose. Tie a knot at one end of the band; then stuff the band with polyester filler. Finish the snowball by tying a knot at the other end. Great balls of fun!

Roxeanne M. Lansing
Rainbow Room Family Day Care
Ballston Spa, NY

Fluffy Flannelboard Pieces

Use the polyester batting used for filling quilts the next time you need to make flannelboard pieces shaped like snowmen, ghosts, or sheep. Simply cut the outlines from the batting; then glue on features cut from felt scraps. The batting sticks firmly to the flannelboard and gives the figures more texture. Your little ones will love this fluffy stuff!

Sedona O'Hara—Three-Year-Olds
University Children's School
California, PA

Sensory Socks

Here's a great tip for making a touch-and-feel teaching aid for youngsters' exploring hands. Insert a plastic cup into the foot of a long tube sock. Gather a collection of objects and corresponding pictures. Place an object in the cup and show several pictures of what the object could be. Have a student volunteer reach into the sock, feel the object, and guess what it is. If his guess is correct, let him choose the next object to go in the cup. Sock it to 'em!

Cheryl B. Cicioni—Three-, Four-, And Five-Year-Olds
Kindernook Preschool
Lancaster, PA

Clocks With Character

Is the clock in your room generic-looking? Jazz it up with this timely tip. Enlarge a seasonal or school-related picture of your choice onto colored bulletin-board paper. Cut out the design and punch a hole in the picture for the clock hanger. Tape the cutout to the wall; then hang your clock. Hickory dickory dock, look at my beautiful clock!

Sue DeMoss—Three-, Four-, And Five-Year-Olds
Maquoketa Head Start
Maquoketa, IA

Hose Hoops

Roll right through your curriculum using these easy-to-make activity hoops. Cut some half-inch PVC water piping into five-foot lengths. Cut a piece of 5/8-inch dowel into two-inch lengths. Apply glue to a dowel piece and insert half of it into one end of a pipe length. Join the ends of the pipe together, around the dowel, and tape the seam with colored tape. Your youngsters will love having their own hoops and your pocketbook will thank you!

Cindy Stewart—Three-, Four-, And Five-Year-Olds
Schuyler Head Start
Schuyler, NE

More Flannel Fun

Double the fun at center time by making this two-sided flannelboard. Cut off the top and bottom flaps of a large, square cardboard box. Then cut off half of two adjoining sides of the box as shown in the diagram. Overlap the two half sides and secure with duct tape to make the board's base. Cover the two large sides of the box with colored felt; then wrap and tape the edges of the felt to the back of each side. Add a basket of flannelboard characters and get ready for some great storytelling!

Cindy Stewart—Three-, Four-, And Five-Year-Olds
Schuyler Head Start
Schuyler, NE

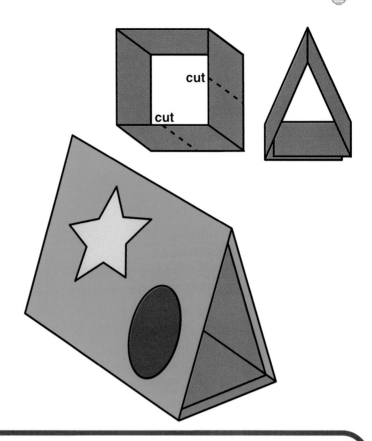

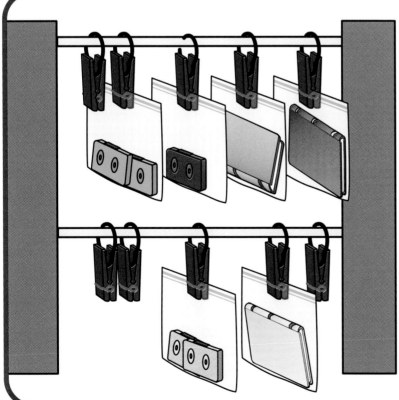

Reading Rack

Store books and accessories together on this handy rack. Place a tension shower-curtain rod between two close walls or two pieces of furniture. Attach shower-curtain rings to the rod; then hang a spring-type clothespin from each ring. Place materials in separate resealable bags and suspend each bag from a clothespin. Books are at your fingertips, ready to be read!

Cindy Stewart—Three-, Four-, And Five-Year-Olds
Schuyler Head Start
Schuyler, NE

Going Nuts Over Good Behavior

Promote positive behavior with this squirrel-themed management idea. To prepare, make a classroom supply of tree cutouts. On each tree trunk, draw five horizontal lines at even intervals. Display the trees on a wall or bulletin board at children's eye level. At the top of each tree, use a clothespin or pushpin to attach a small paper bag or berry basket. For each child, duplicate a squirrel pattern from page 148 on gray construction paper. Cut out the squirrel, label it with the child's name, and laminate it for durability. Post each squirrel at the base of a different tree.

With each day of good behavior, have the child move his squirrel up to the next line. Reward the child with an acorn when his squirrel reaches the fifth line; then return the squirrel to the bottom of the tree. Once several acorns are collected, invite the child to cash in his acorns for prizes. For example, an eraser might cost two acorns and a small toy might cost four acorns. You'll have a lot of bright eyes and bushy tails scampering for nuts by following classroom rules!

Cynthia Corey—Gr. K, Heritage Christian School, Canton, OH

Picture-Perfect Behavior

Getting little ones to follow class rules is a snap with this idea. Enlarge the camera pattern on page 147. Color, cut out, and mount the camera along with your class rules on a bulletin board. Title your display "Picture-Perfect Behavior." Have an instant camera at your fingertips to snap photos of students exhibiting good behavior. Add these photos to the display near the appropriate rule. When all students have a picture on the display, celebrate with a special treat. For more meaning, invite the principal to the party. Smile—your students are behaving!

Michelle L. Schaal
St. Elmo Elementary, St. Elmo, IL

PICTURE-PERFECT BEHAVIOR

1. Listen
2. Keep Hands To Yourself
3. Use Kind Words
4. Share

Child In Charge

Have students take responsibility in making sure all materials are put away after center time. Each day designate a child to be in charge of supervising center cleanup. Explain that her job is to carefully inspect each center area to make sure all items have been returned to their proper places. For added effect, provide a pair of oversized eyeglass frames for her to wear for extra help in examining centers. Children will love being the boss when their turn comes, and you'll love not having to clean up misplaced materials.

Debi Hussell—Gr. K, Central Elementary, Pt. Pleasant, WV

Sticker Solution

Do stickers frequently fall off deserving children before they make it home? Try these sticker books instead. Staple several sheets of construction paper together; then label the front of each book with a different child's name. Each time a sticker is awarded to a child, encourage him to put it in his sticker book. Send the books home periodically to be "oohed" and "aahed" over by parents. At the end of the year each child should have quite a sticky selection!

Debbie Brown—Pre-K, Corson Park Daycare, Millville, NJ

The Tissue Issue

Avoid disruptive trips to the tissue box with this handy tip. Instead of requesting large boxes of tissues at the beginning of the year, ask parents to send individual packs. Place an individual pack of tissues on each table for several children to share. Runny noses can be caught without the child leaving his seat!

Amy Scott—Gr. K
St. Augustine School
Napoleon, OH

Name Caps

Choosing volunteers for special tasks is easy and fair when you use this selection method. Obtain a classroom supply of plastic milk-jug caps. Using a permanent marker, label each cap with a different child's name. For extra protection against ink fading or rubbing off, apply a layer of acrylic spray to the labeled side of the caps. Store the name caps in a covered margarine tub. When a helper is needed, simply shake the container and draw a name. Promote reading readiness by allowing children to pick and read classmates' names from the tub, too!

Doreen O'Neil—Gr. K
St. Philomena
Portsmouth, RI

Sing To Me!

Make positive discipline sound like music to little ones' ears. Instead of pointing out inappropriate behaviors, sing a little tune praising the children who are following directions and behaving in a positive way. It's sure to get the attention of *all* your students and keep you happy as well!

Debi Hussell—Gr. K, Central Elementary, Pt. Pleasant, WV

Linking Kids To Kindness

Instill the virtue of kindness in your students as they watch this kindness chain grow and grow. Each time you see a kind act by a student, reward him by helping him add a link to a paper chain. Hang the chain in the room for all to see; then share with the rest of the children the kind deed you witnessed. Your classroom will soon be wrapped up in the kindness chain!

Janice Leidal—Gr. K
Early Childhood Center
West Fargo, ND

Give Me Five!

Use a programmed hand cutout to remind youngsters of good learning skills. Introduce the hand by reading the words on each finger and discussing how that particular action helps in learning. For younger students, include an illustration with each direction on a finger. After the hand is introduced, display it near your circle-time area. When circle time arrives, cue your youngsters by saying, "Give me five." Have them show you that they are attentive by holding up one of their hands. They're ready to learn!

Rhonda Lehmann—Gr. K
Morningside Elementary
Great Falls, MT

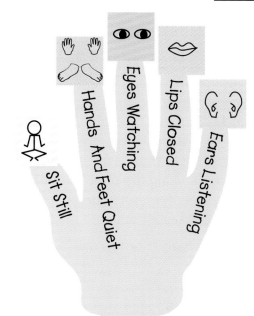

A Thankful Moment

Promote good manners at snacktime with this gracious idea. After everyone has been served, instruct your children to hold hands and recite the following verse. Make this a daily ritual to keep little snackers from nibbling prematurely.

Preschool is fun.
I like to learn and play.
My friend, [child's name] brought our snack today.
Thank you, [child's name]!

Patricia Shemwell—Preschool, Hickory Hills Preschool, Hickory Hills, IL

Listening Ears

Develop listening skills in your little ones with this fun tip. Wear a pair of plastic, oversized ears during storytime and while you're giving directions. These funny ear pieces will remind youngsters to perk up their own ears to hear all the information. For added fun, invite a super listener to wear the ears during a group time. Your youngsters will love this incentive to be all ears!

Debi Hussell—Gr. K
Central Elementary
Pt. Pleasant, WV

Dust-Buster Buddies

Children needing a little extra attention will love helping out with a dust-buster buddy. To make one, glue large wiggle eyes onto a washcloth; then use puffy fabric paint to draw a smile. Have children take turns using the dust-buster to dust shelves, centers, and cubbies. Who ya gonna call? Dust-busters!

Jennifer L. Hipps—Three-Year-Olds
Fairfield Enrichment Center
High Point, NC

Conduct Clip-Ons

Reward good conduct with these easy-to-make conduct clip-ons. Cut a class supply of pictures from greeting cards; then glue each picture to a different wooden, spring-loaded clothespin. Store the clip-ons on a length of yarn hanging within children's reach. As a student shows appropriate behavior, invite her to choose a clip-on to wear. Challenge your little ones to have a perfect day in which there will be no clips left on the yarn. An empty strand of yarn definitely deserves a special treat!

Kay Dawson—Gr. K, B. C. Charles Elementary, Newport News, VA

A "Re-bark-able" Rinsing Dish

Cleaning up goes to the dogs with this handy tip. When completing a group painting project, use dog bowls as rinsing cups for paintbrushes. The bowls are sturdy and won't tip over. Woof, woof!

Laurie Birt—Gr. K
Belinder School
Prairie Village, KS

Class-Activity Clock

Ease children's separation anxiety by tracking the day with an activity clock. Cut a large circle from poster board. Use a marker to divide it into the same number of triangles as activities in your school day. Starting at the top of the circle, work clockwise and label each triangle with a portion of your daily schedule. Cut pictures from magazines and catalogs that illustrate each activity; then glue them to the corresponding triangles. Cut a clock hand from colored poster board and attach it with a brad to the center of the circle.

To use, move the hand around the clock as each activity is completed. Little ones will soon learn the schedule and be reassured of when it's time to go home.

Susan Nickolson—Two-Year-Olds
Cumberland Presbyterian Church
Scottsboro, AL

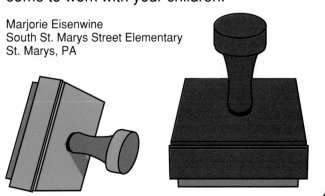

Rubber-Stamp Nametags

Need nametags in a hurry? Stamp a sheet of plain mailing labels with a rubber-stamp design; then write a different student's name on each label. Mailing labels stick to clothing better than most store-bought nametags and they're less expensive. You'll be ready in a flash for any special visitors or substitutes who come to work with your children.

Marjorie Eisenwine
South St. Marys Street Elementary
St. Marys, PA

Library Coupons

Encourage children's responsibility for bringing back library books on time with this incentive. In advance, cut out small pictures from patterns on Con-Tact® covering. Stick each picture onto a different 3" x 2" piece of tagboard. Write "coupon" on each piece. Explain to your youngsters that each week they bring back their library books on time, they will receive a coupon. Then tell them that these coupons can be collected and traded for prizes in the treasure box or for another special treat of your choice. Forgotten books will soon be a memory!

Tina Butterbaugh—Gr. K
His Majesty's Learning Center
Lexington, KY

Picture-Cue Helpers

Here's a helpful tip for working with students needing extra help with following directions. Prepare small, square picture-cue cards like those shown for common directions that you give. Attach the hook side of a strip of Velcro® to the top edge of the student's desk. Then attach loop side pieces of Velcro® to the backs of each picture cue. After you've given the class verbal directions, stick the direction cards to the Velcro® in order. This modification will help foster children's independence and will keep you from constantly repeating directions. It's a winning situation!

Barbara D. Triplett—Gr. K
M. E. Boone Elementary
San Antonio, TX

Write

Color Cut Glue

After While, Crocodile!

Say good-bye to your children each day with these rollicking rhymes. Start by placing one animal picture and rhyme at the top of the exiting door's frame. Demonstrate the rhyme with its motion. At the end of the day, have children perform the rhyme with you. Add another picture and rhyme under the previous one each week—adding some creative rhymes of your own—until the pictures touch the floor. Each day go through the entire repertoire. Your little ones will leave the room all smiles!

Bye, bye, butterfly! *(Wave good-bye.)*
See ya soon, raccoon! *(Point to your eyes.)*
Give a hug, bug! *(Hug yourself.)*
Toot-a-loo, kangaroo! *(Hop around in a small circle.)*
Take a bow, cow! *(Take a big bow.)*

Kerry Zarlengo—Four- And Five-Year-Olds
Our Lady Of Fatima School
Lakewood, CO

Bye, bye, butterfly!

Toot-a-loo, kangaroo!

Take a bow, cow!

No More Sticky Tables

Recycle old greeting cards to make these handy mats for gluing activities. Cut several pictures from cards and glue them onto a piece of poster board. Cover the front of the board with clear Con-Tact® covering, leaving about two inches to be wrapped around to the back. When an activity calls for glue, instruct each child to get a mat to put under her work first. Excess glue is caught on the mat and not the tabletop! Wipe the mats periodically with a warm, soapy cloth. Glue be gone!

Tina Butterbaugh—Gr. K
His Majesty's Learning Center
Lexington, KY

Helpful Hints

Here are a few quick tips for some common household items that can be helpful in your classroom!

Washcloths: Make an ice pack by wetting a washcloth, inserting it into a resealable bag, and freezing it. This is a softer way to soothe bumps and bruises than using regular ice.

Coffee Filters: Use these as individual snack holders. They're perfect for a handful of goodies and are very inexpensive.

Cardboard Tubes: Send home important papers in these tubes. Simply roll up papers and stick them inside. Labeling the tube with a name and stickers is sure to get parents to look inside!

Connie Powell—Early Childhood Special Education
Cloud Elementary
Wichita, KS

Center Time!

Name	GLITTER		books
Chondi	❄		❄
Kendra		❄	
Alex		❄	❄
Philip	❄		
Lisa			❄
Jesse		❄	
Carla		❄	
Seth	❄	❄	
Rachel			❄
Zach		❄	❄

Structuring Centers

Encourage children to complete tasks at various learning centers. Make a class chart with several empty columns as shown. Cut out a few stars from construction paper. Laminate the chart and stars for durability. Prepare three signs for each center—a large one to post in the center; a medium-size one for the chalkboard; and a small one for the class chart. Provide access to a seasonal rubber stamp and a washable ink pad.

To implement this management method, post the medium-size center signs on the chalkboard to let students know which centers are open. Place a star beside each center sign that is a "must-do" activity. Post the corresponding small center signs in the empty boxes at the top of the class chart. Children will know when they arrive which centers are open and what they need to do. As each child finishes an activity, have him go to the chart and stamp the appropriate column beside his name. At the end of the day, the chart can be wiped clean and reprogrammed. Managing center time using this method gives your children more responsibility and independence and frees you up for more facilitating.

Lauren Egizio—Substitute Teacher
Easton Public Schools
Easton, MA

A "Beary" Nice Line

Make lining up more fun and organized with this fuzzy tip. At lineup time, give a stuffed teddy bear to a child who is sitting quietly. As he lines up, instruct him to pass the bear to another quiet child. The bear keeps passing from child to child until everyone is in line. The last youngster to get the bear passes it back to you. What a "beary" nice line!

Melissa L. Olinger—Four-Year-Olds
Little Friends Preschool
Denver, CO

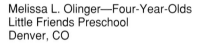

A Slice Of Good Behavior

A Slice Of Good Behavior

Challenge your whole class to have good days with this fruity incentive. Display a watermelon cutout. At the end of each day, put one seed on the cutout for a well-behaved class. When ten seeds have been added, celebrate with a real watermelon snack. Juicy, juicy, juicy!

Amy Pierce—Pre-K
Pierce Private Day School
Irving, TX

A Cool Idea

Foster your home-school connection with a take-home cooler loaded with cool learning activities. Pack a plastic cooler with a notebook and a variety of interesting materials and manipulatives related to a specific skill or theme—such as plastic animal counters, a counting book, counting beads, and a counting game. Include a "cooler critter"—a toy penguin or polar bear—to accompany the package. Attach a label printed with "Cool Things To Do" to the cooler handle. If desired, tape an inventory list of the contents to the inside of the cooler lid. Then invite each youngster, in turn, to carry the cooler home. Encourage him to share the activities with his family, then dictate his experiences for his parent to write in the notebook. After every child has had a turn to take home the cooler, replace its contents with different items; then send it home again with each child. What a cool way to keep families involved with their children's learning!

Janet Matthews—Gr. K, Riverhills Elementary, Temple Terrace, FL

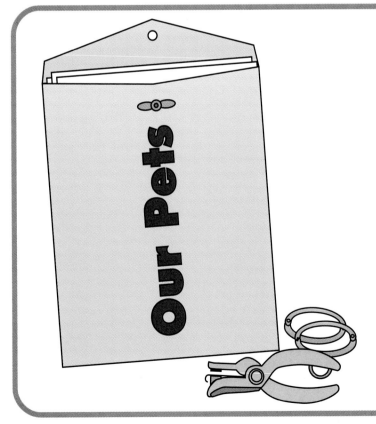

Proud Parent Publishers

Save time while using a valuable resource by recruiting parent volunteers to assemble student-made books. After students make their book pages, package the pages and binding materials in a large envelope. Then ask your parent volunteers to assemble the books for the class. If a parent is willing to help, but can't come to school, send the package home with her child or mail her the package along with a self-addressed, stamped envelope. Students will enjoy receiving the completed books and parents will be proud to have helped in the publishing process.

Sandra Armstrong—Gr. K
Woodrow Wilson
East Peoria, IL

Teddy-Bear Ties

Let an adorable teddy bear and a journal provide the ties for a successful home-school connection. Have the class adopt and name a cute teddy bear to be your class mascot. Put the bear, along with a journal, in a special bag or handled box. Have each child in turn take the bear home with him overnight. Ask him to have his parent write in the journal his dictation about his real or imaginary experiences with the bear. Encourage the child to invite his family members to help him illustrate his journal page. When the child returns the bag to school, invite him to share his adventures with the class. After the journal pages are complete, add the book to your class library. Youngsters will find this home-school tie-in to be "bear-y" rewarding.

Tricia Draper—Gr. K, Millarville Community School
Turner Valley, Alberta

Packed For Parents

Send home a class project packed with powerful parent input! Each month, prepare a package by filling a large manila envelope or zippered storage bag with a theme-related book and the necessary materials for completing a related activity—such as completing a page for a class book or creating a zoo animal. Enclose an explanation and directions for the activity. Have a different child take home the package each night to share with her parents. When each child returns the package activity to school, ask her to tell the class about it. After every child has returned her completed activity, compile the individual items into a class project—such as a class book or zoo display. These packages will produce pleasurable parent participation in each child's education.

Margaret Smith—Gr. K, St. Augustine, Troy, NY

Hooray For Helpers!

Two, four, six, eight. Who do we appreciate? Parent helpers, of course! To make the flow of your valuable helpers coming into and out of your classroom more efficient and less disruptive, list the jobs to be completed by parent volunteers on a dry-erase board. Then create separate packages containing the materials and directions needed to perform each job. Place the packages in a designated area. When a volunteer arrives, he simply checks the board for his job, retrieves the package, and sets to work. After he completes the job, he will place the package in another designated area, then wipe that job off the board. As a token of your appreciation, invite each parent volunteer to take an individually wrapped piece of candy from a dish labeled "Hooray For Helpers!"

Ellen S. Bruno—Special Education
Esta Fowler—Gr. K
Rio Rancho Elementary, Rio Rancho, NM

Things To Do:
★ Cut laminated pictures apart.
★ Put together student books.

Hooray For Helpers!

Create A Story

This story-in-the-making will keep both students and parents anticipating the next chapter. To begin, purchase a blank, hardcover book; then write a story-starter on the first page of the book. Put the book in a special bag with a stuffed animal to serve as the book guardian. Then have each child, in turn, take home the book and ask his parent to help him add a chapter to the story. When each child returns the book, read his chapter to the class. Continue to rotate the book from home to home until all the pages are filled. Then duplicate a class quantity of each page, and assemble a copy of the book for each child. Encourage youngsters to take home their books to read with their families.

Susan Schneider—Gr. K, Durham Elementary, Durham, NY

Please return to Ms. Schneider

Dear Mr. and Mrs. Berringer,

I just wanted to drop you a line to tell you how well Kimberley is doing at school! She is a wonderful listener!

Ms. Steele

Mr. and Mrs. Berringer
123 Maple Street
Tree City, FL

Postcards With A Plus

Promote home-school communications by periodically sending postcards with positive comments. Each week write and send a separate postcard to the parents of several different students. Include only positive information on the cards—such as praising the child for reciting his alphabet or demonstrating friendship to his classmates. When parents receive such good news in the mail, they'll be popping with pride!

Kimberley Berringer—Gr. K
Dillard Street Elementary
Apopka, FL

Seasonal Suggestions

'Tis the season to do something fun with your child! This is the message parents will get when they receive a newsletter filled with seasonal activities to share with their children. To learn about family-oriented activities and upcoming events, check your local newspaper and publications from community service organizations. Then include information about these events—such as the place, date, time, and a brief description of the activity—in a seasonal class newsletter. Send home a copy of the newsletter with each child, encouraging him to spend family time participating in some of the suggested activities. Creating awareness of special events can create some memorable family times for your little ones.

Mary Frances Casey—Preschool
Chatterbox Day School, E. Islip, NY

Class News

Fall Is Here!

Enjoy some of these fall events with your family:

Apple Picking at Appleby's Farm in East City daily. Pick your own and pay at the gate.

Pumpkin Thumping

The Pumpkin Place at 654 State Rd. in Middleton. Every weekend in October. Learn all about pumpkins and play some unique pumpkin games.

Family Big Book

Emphasize the concept of family with this family-made class big book. Cut out a large, but simple, tagboard house shape—or book page—for each child. Attach a note to each page, requesting that the family work together to glue photos of family members on one side of the page (or draw them). Ask them to write the names of places they visit in the community—such as the library, grocery store, or a fast-food restaurant—on the other side of the page. Then have each child take home a page to complete with his family. After all the children return their pages, bind the pages together between house-shaped covers to create a big book. Write "Our Families" on the front cover; then share the book with youngsters. Discuss the similarities and differences among families and the places they visit.

We like to go to:

Southside Library

Mahoney's Burgers

Gina's Playroom

Barrington Food Mart

The Trent Family

Gina Mahoney—Three-Year-Olds, Children's Preschool Workshop, Barrington, IL

Helpful Hints For Conferences

Create a positive, relaxing atmosphere for parent conferences with some of these useful suggestions. Arrange a display of student work and provide light refreshments for parents in the conference waiting area. Ease each parent's anxiety during the conference by sitting at a round table and having samples of his child's work available for a quick visual reference. Respond to the parent's questions and concerns in a positive manner. Immediately after the conference, be sure to jot down any interesting or useful bits of information gathered from the parent about his child. Who says parent-teacher conferences can't be enjoyable and educational for everyone?

Seema Gersten
Harkham Hillel Hebrew Academy, Beverly Hills, CA

A Cheer For _Cheryl_

Rah! Rah! Rah!
Sis boom bah!
See what I know!
Rah! Rah! Rah!

Color: _orange_
Shape: _circle_
Letter(s): _D_
Number(s): _3_
Other: _above, below_

©1997 The Education Center, Inc. • TEC810

Rootin'-Tootin' Progress Reports

Send home these monthly progress reports to cheer youngsters and their parents for their learning efforts! For each child, duplicate a copy of the progress report form on page 147; then write in the appropriate information for each student on a separate form. Have each child take her progress report home to share with her parents. Rah! Rah! Rah! Sis boom bah! See what I know! Rah! Rah! Rah!

Cheryl B. Cicioni—Four- And Five-Year-Olds
Kindernook Preschool, Lancaster, PA

Family Fun In A Briefcase

Strengthen home-school ties with a donated or inexpensive briefcase filled with family writing activities. Obtain a briefcase and pack it with a variety of writing utensils, an assortment of paper, a picture book, a journal, and a parent note explaining the purpose of the briefcase. Invite each student, in turn, to carry the briefcase home overnight. Ask the child to involve his family members in reading the book to him, then helping him illustrate a journal page about his favorite part of the story. If desired, each family member might also create his own illustration using the materials in the briefcase. Suggest that the child tell about his illustration and have a family member write his dictation in the journal. Then, when the child returns the briefcase, invite him to share his—and any family member's—illustrations with the class. Now that's fun family involvement! Case closed!

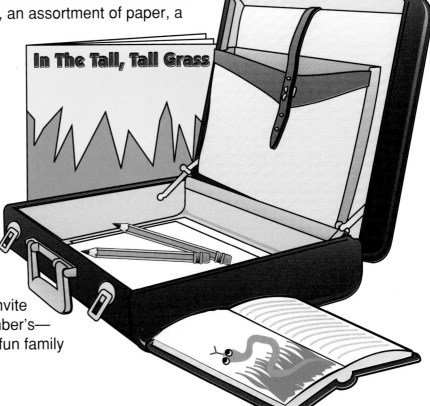

In The Tall, Tall Grass

Debi Hussell—Five-Year-Olds, Central Elementary
Pt. Pleasant, WV

Creativity For Charity

Give youngsters the opportunity to give of themselves with an art show for charity. Encourage each child to create a special work of art using materials of his choice. Display the masterpieces in an art show. Then invite co-workers, parents, and friends to purchase the artwork by placing anonymous donations in a designated basket. Use the funds collected from the art sale to purchase food or other items for a needy family or to donate to a charitable organization. Creativity for charity—everyone wins!

Patricia Shemwell—Preschool
Hickory Hills Pk. District Preschool
Hickory Hills, IL

Bring It On Home

Extra! Extra! Parents can read all about thematic units and skills their youngsters are learning with a class newsletter. At the end of each week or unit lesson, prepare a newsletter to include a section on parent-child activities related to the skills and concepts learned. Send home a copy of the letter with each child, encouraging his family to try some of the suggested activities. This easy form of communicating with parents is a great way for youngsters to bring home their learning.

Kim Richman—Three-Year-Olds
The Learning Zone
Des Moines, IA

Warm Hands, Warm Heart

Youngsters will experience warm hearts when they donate mittens to warm the hands of some needy children. Set up an artificial tree or a paper tree display in your classroom. Ask students to bring in new or slightly used pairs of mittens to decorate the tree. Before the holidays, donate the mittens to a charitable organization to be given to needy children in your area. It feels so good to share the warmth!

Patricia Shemwell—Preschool

A Family Garden In Bloom

Youngsters' pride in their families will blossom when they help make this display. Send a large bulletin-board flower cutout home with each child. Instruct the child to ask his family to help decorate the cutout using materials of their choice—such as glitter, crayons, seeds, doilies, magazine pictures, or yarn. When the child returns his flower, invite him to tell the class about each family member's contribution to its decorations. Then display all the flowers, with construction-paper stems and leaves, in a hallway for students and their families to admire and enjoy.

Kay Dawson—Gr. K
B. C. Charles Elementary, Newport News, Va

Year In Review

Compile all those photographs that you've taken throughout the year into a special yearbook for youngsters. Near the end of the year, assemble photos of your students engaged in daily routines, field trips, and other special projects onto pages in scrapbook fashion. Sequence the pages; then add brief quotes and lines of text, if desired. Duplicate a set of the pages for each child; then bind each set between construction-paper covers. Write "Our Year In Review" on the front cover of each book. Give each child a copy of the class yearbook to take home as a keepsake.

Mary Langford—Gr. K, St. Agnes School, Butler, WI

The Write Connection

Don't cut the lines between home and school just because summer has arrived! Keep in touch with your students and their families with this idea. Early in the summer, send each of your former students a special greeting and a photo taken during the previous school year. Enclose a self-addressed, stamped envelope and a request that the child ask a family member to help him write back to you. This is just the "write" idea to keep in touch *and* to encourage a family writing venture over the summer!

Connie Powell—Gr. K, Special Education
Cloud Elementary, Wichita, KS

Dear Todd,

I hope you are having a great summer. I thought you would like to keep this picture. It reminds me

Mrs. Powell
9981 West Ave.
Wichita, KS

Now *That's* A Calendar!

Calendar concepts will make a *big* impression with this display! Cover a bulletin board with black paper. Use masking tape to divide the board into 35 equally sized boxes. Cut large numerals from colored construction paper. Then refer to a current month's calendar to attach them in the correct boxes on the display with pushpins.

Use the large calendar display for practice with counting, exploring days and weeks, recognizing numerals, and planning special events. Highlight the current date with a different colored construction-paper circle. Change the border and the color of the numerals frequently to fit seasonal or thematic units.

Sue DeMoss—Three-, Four-, And Five-Year-Olds, Maquoketa II Head Start, Maquoketa, IA

Dynamite Doors

Bulletin boards and walls aren't the only places for displays. Put them on your doors, too! Door displays can help create a wonderful learning environment. For example, when teaching a bear unit, create a display that will make children feel they're walking into a bear cave. Or dress your door to resemble the entrance to a candy house during the holidays. The possibilities are endless, so open the door to your imagination!

Adapted from an idea by Sandra O'Connell—Gr. K
M. M. Pierce
Remington, VA

Poster Profiles

Get to know your little ones as you build this train of personalities. Help each child complete the six activities listed below. Arrange and glue his lists and pictures on a large sheet of colored construction paper. Add two black construction-paper wheels so the paper resembles a train car. Connect your group's train cars together with black paper strips and display the train across the walls of your room. Add a large train-engine cutout to the front of the lineup that's titled with your class name or room number. Youngsters and adults alike will enjoy this getting-to-know-you choo choo!

Items for each train car:
1. Individual photo of the child
2. List of child's physical characteristics (eye color, height, weight, age, etc.)
3. Child's illustration of his family
4. Several magazine pictures of the child's favorite things
5. Child's illustration of what he wants to be when he grows up
6. Child's dictation describing three wishes

Nancy Hamilton—Four-Year-Olds, Discovery Days, Allen, TX

A Shapely Caterpillar

Reinforce shape recognition with this shapely display. Provide your children with tagboard shape patterns. Have each child trace and cut out a shape of her choice from colored construction paper. Mount these shapes side by side, forming a curvy line on a bulletin board. Add a head with antennae to the front of the line. Use a marker to draw legs and feet below each shape. Invite volunteers to pick a tagboard pattern and find its matching shapes on the caterpillar.

Tammy Skinner—Gr. K, Carver Elementary, Pinetops, NC

Wonderful Windows

Is your classroom without windows? Or do you wish you had more? Here's a fun display that gives the illusion that the great outdoors is just a step away. Take the children on a quick walk around your school or center. Once back indoors, divide your class into small groups. Give each group a large square of bulletin-board paper.

Invite them to draw and color an outdoor scene that's appropriate for the current season. Cut strips of brown bulletin-board paper and create window frames over each picture. Attach the mock windows to your classroom walls. Be sure to change scenery with the seasons. Best of all, these windows require no washing!

Deborah Smalling—Gr. K
Austin Parkway Elementary
Sugar Land, TX

Environment Wallpaper

Give your youngsters early success at reading by covering a wall with a collage of environmental print. Ask children and parents to bring in empty boxes from cereals, snacks, and other foods. Cut out the front panel of each box and attach it to a wall. Provide a pointer so that children can practice reading the wall to one another. Their confidence will soar with this reading success!

Teresa Edison—Three- And Four-Year-Olds
Luther Hospital Child Care Center
Eau Claire, WI

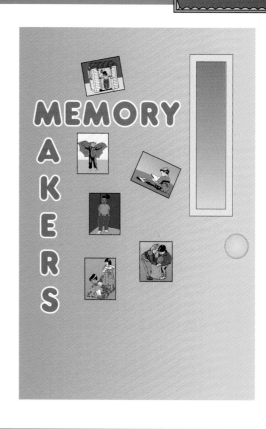

Memory Makers

Use your classroom door as a year-long scrapbook. Attach pictures that you take throughout the year to your door, along with the title "Memory Makers." What a great way to show parents and school visitors the many precious moments in your class.

Amy Pierce—Pre-K
Pierce Private Day School
Irving, TX

Wall Of Felt

Turn a section of your classroom wall into an awesome teaching tool. Cover a section of the wall with a wide strip of felt. Attach the felt so that one end is almost touching the floor. Divide this fantastic felt wall for three uses. Display a flannelboard set at the top that correlates with your current unit of study. Use the middle section and other flannelboard pieces to reinforce skills—such as patterning and counting—in a whole-group setting. Invite children to use the bottom section as a storytelling center. Now that's making the most of your wall space!

Kimberly Leite—Student Teacher
Southwestern Adventist College
Keene, TX

Interactive Bus

Add a spark to the traditional "Wheels On The Bus" song with this interactive display. Enlarge a bus pattern, color it, then cut off its wheels and lights. Glue the bus frame to a large sheet of paper. Find and cut out pictures of children, adults, a driver, and babies. Laminate the bus and all the accessory pieces. Attach the hook side of a self-adhesive Velcro® dot to each space on the bus that needs a cutout. Attach the loop side of a self-adhesive Velcro® dot to the back of each cutout. As you sing each verse of the song with your children, invite volunteers to place the correct picture on the bus. Your little ones are sure to ask for another ride!

Robin Little Birney—Special Education
Carl Dwire Jr. School
Oxnard, CA

Fishing For Helpers

Bait a bulletin board to display your classroom helpers. Cover a board with blue paper and frame it with a fish border. Duplicate the fish pattern on page 149 on colored construction paper for each of your classroom duties; then duplicate the worm pattern on page 149 onto brown construction paper for each child. Cut out all the fish and worms. Label each fish with a different duty and each worm with a different child's name. Staple the fish to the board; then pin a worm to the board in front of each fish's mouth. Store extra worms in a resealable bag near the board. For added effect, tape a wooden dowel (fishing rod) with yarn and a pipe-cleaner hook to the board. Need a line leader? Go fish!

Lisa Willis—Pre-K
Talent House Private School
Fairfax, VA

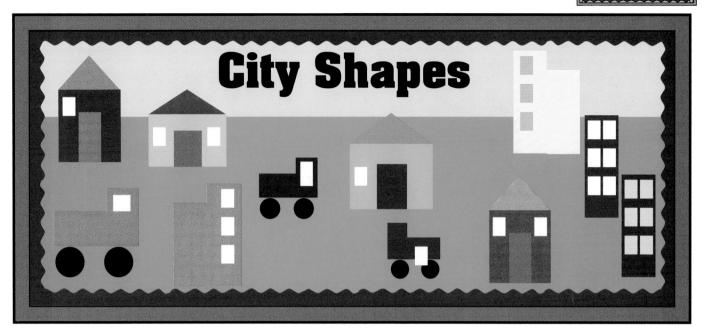

Little imaginations will run wild with this cityscape made from shapes. Cover a bulletin board with green and blue paper as shown. Invite children to draw and cut out their own shapes or use precut construction-paper shapes to create vehicles, buildings, homes, signs, or anything else seen in the city. It will be interesting to see how each child's creation helps this display take shape!

Nancy Umbaugh—Four-Year-Olds, Faith Lutheran School, North Palm Beach, FL

A class supply of construction-paper squares will make balloon baskets for this high-flying display! Have each child trace a balloon pattern onto construction paper, cut it out, and decorate it. Glue each child's picture on a different basket; then write his name below his picture. Attach each basket to its decorated balloon by taping the ends of two yarn pieces to the back of each item. Display the balloons with cotton-ball clouds. Up, up, and away!

Peggy Miller—Four- And Five-Year-Olds, Rabbit Hill Nursery School, Springfield, PA

Display some social studies curriculum in your classroom. Prepare a bulletin board with different types of home cutouts—such as a tepee, an apartment building, a house, and an igloo. Cut out a square—or window—in one of the dwellings for each child. Attach individual photos behind the cutouts. Enlarge the plane and pilot pattern on page 150; then make a title banner trailing behind the plane as shown.

Mary Langford—Gr. K, St. Agnes School, Butler, WI

Decorate a hallway board to depict a bear habitat that will stay up the whole year, reflecting seasonal changes. Include a fact box that explains the bear's activity during the specific season. For a fun twist, dress the bear for Halloween and Easter. Decorate her cave for Christmas. Invite your students to make valentines for her. And in the spring, bring the bear out of her cave with… SURPRISE…bear cubs!

Dawn Schollenberger—Gr. K, Mary S. Shoemaker School, Woodstown, NJ

A string of red Christmas lights creates a wide realm of possibilities for lighting up a bulletin-board display the whole year. Tape the lights to your board; then add the decor. Try shiny apples in September, glowing reindeer noses in December, radiant May flowers, or come up with your own bright ideas!

Kendra J. Olson—Gr. K, Seneca Grade School, Seneca, IL

Encourage making new friends with this poem display. Help each child trace and cut out his handprint from gold or silver metallic wrapping paper. Label the child's handprint with his name or photo. Staple the gold and silver handprints into a circle on your board. Inside of the circle, copy the words to the poem. Friends forever!

Make new friends, but keep the old.
One is silver and the other gold.
A circle is round, it has no end.
That's how long I want to be your friend.

Gina Mahony—Four- And Five-Year-Olds
Children's Preschool Workshop
Barrington, IL

Three Cheers For South Elementary School

Crank up some school spirit with your next hallway display. Title your board "Three cheers for _____!" Fill in the blank with either your school name or the grade level you teach. Hang cutouts of three of your favorite characters on the board and attach real pom-poms to their hands. Hip, hip, hooray!

Darlene M. Martin—Pre-K, South Elementary School, Hingham, MA

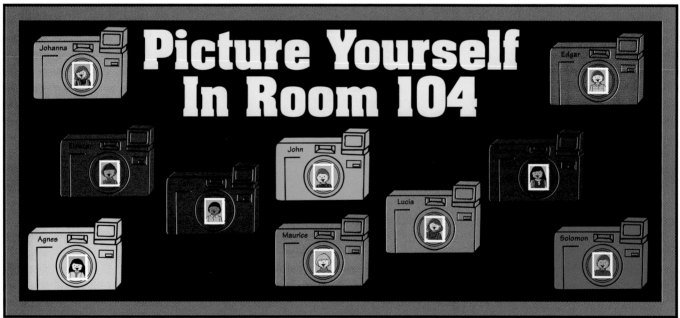

Welcome students with this photo display. Duplicate the camera pattern on page 147 for each child. Obtain a photo of each child (taken during a home visit or on "Meet-Your-Teacher" day). Attach a photo to each camera lens; then label the camera with the child's name. Arrange the cameras on the bulletin board around the title. Have an instant camera on hand to snap pictures of any new students when they arrive.

Michelle L. Schaal, St. Elmo Elementary, St. Elmo, IL

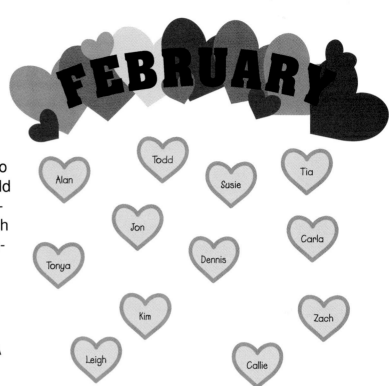

Save some wall space to display the month's name with seasonal decor. For example, use multi-colored paper hearts to display the word "February." Ask each child to write her name on a sheet from a heart-shaped notepad. Use these hearts to finish the monthly display. In October use pumpkins. In January use snowmen and snowflakes. Drawing youngsters' attention to this display will help with their recognition of the months.

Sandra O'Connell—Gr. K, M. M. Pierce, Remington, VA

October

Show the passage of time to your youngsters with this artwork timeline. Each month label a sentence strip with the month's name. Tape this strip to your wall. Under the strip, mount a few samples of artwork completed that month. Display the months side by side across your room. Little ones will love remembering what was done and parents will be fascinated at the progress that their children have made.

Annette Hensley—Three-, Four-, And Five-Year-Olds
Hillcrest School, Huffman Estates, IL

Cut eight long lengths of white yarn; then tie them into a knot at one end. Pin the knot to the center of a black background. Stretch out the other ends and pin them to the board. Spiral another long length of yarn around the web, pinning it to the board at each intersection with the other pieces. Invite each child to make a spider to add to the display by using half of a Styrofoam® ball, paint, pipe cleaners, and wiggle eyes.

Tricia Draper—Gr. K, Millarville Community School, Turner Valley, Alberta

Create a puzzling pumpkin patch on a bulletin board. First cut leaf shapes from green paper. Staple the leaves intertwined with green, curling ribbon to the board. Enlarge and duplicate a pumpkin pattern from page 149 for each child. Have the child color and cut out his pumpkin. Staple only the top of the pumpkin to the board. Under each child's pumpkin, attach a picture of him holding a real pumpkin. Guess who?

Shirley Coulter Ericson—Pre-K, Cornwall Children's Center, Cornwall, PA

Give your students' Santas a little insight about their children's Christmas wishes. Have each child draw and dictate something she hopes Santa will bring to her. Staple a piece of Christmas wrap—the same size as the paper—to the picture's top edge. Invite the child to attach a self-adhesive bow and gift tag to the paper. Pin these gifts to a bulletin board under a Christmas tree cutout. Santa Claus is comin' to town!

Linda Dean—Three- And Four-Year-Olds, Presbyterian Early Enrichment Program, Beulaville, NC

Prepare this wintry board by making a frozen pond with aluminum foil. Glue cotton around the foil to resemble snow. Add a background of shimmering pines to create the perfect scene for skaters! Duplicate a pattern from page 151 for each child. Have him color his skater and add facial features to match his physical traits—such as eye and hair color. Cut out and staple these colorful characters to your scenery. Let it snow!

Nancy P. Emerick—Gr. K, St. Raphael School, Pittsburgh, PA

Trace a large red and a smaller white heart shape onto construction paper for each child. Have the child cut out these hearts, then glue the smaller heart inside the larger heart. Assist each child in tracing and cutting the outline of her hand from skin-toned paper. Fold the middle and ring fingers towards the palm and secure them with glue. Then glue the entire hand cutout to the center of the hearts. Arrange the heart cutouts around the title as shown.

Melissa L. Olinger—Four-Year-Olds, Little Friends Preschool, Denver, CO

Duplicate the patterns on page 152 for each child. (Reproduce the chick pattern on yellow construction paper and the egg pattern on white construction paper.) Cut different colored 4 1/2" x 3" rectangles to make books. Have each child cut out the patterns, then draw eyes and a beak on his chick. Write the child's favorite title on his book. Assist him in gluing the chick, book, and egg pieces together as shown. Staple these fuzzy readers to a springtime board. Peep, peep!

Regina M. Smith—Gr. K, Glenwood Elementary, Princeton, WV

After discussing the three Rs (reduce, reuse, recycle), ask children to bring in lightweight items from home that can be recycled. Assist each child in tracing and cutting out his handprint twice, once on blue paper and once on green paper. Arrange the handprints on a bulletin board to resemble a big globe. Attach the recyclable items that were brought in around the globe.

Lisa Cohen—Gr. K, Laurel Plains Elementary, New City, NY

Compliment your little ones with this lip-lickin' display. Enlarge the honey-pot pattern on page 153 for the center of the bulletin board. Then write the title on the front of the pot. Cut out this pot and staple it to your board. Duplicate the honey-pot pattern on page 153 for each child. Invite her to color and cut out her pattern. Label each cutout with the child's name and attach her photo. Mount the honey pots around the title.

Deborah Koharbash—Three-Year-Olds, Hillel Academy, Pittsburgh, PA

Cover a bulletin board with blue and brown paper. Cut a few vines, stems, leaves, and roots from construction paper and mount them on the board. Provide a variety of vegetable-shaped cutouts. Invite students to sponge-paint the cutouts to resemble tomatoes, potatoes, carrots, and other vegetables. Encourage each child to pin his painted veggie on the board where it grows—above or below the ground.

Laura Fitz—Three- And Four-Year-Olds, Even Start, Essex, MD

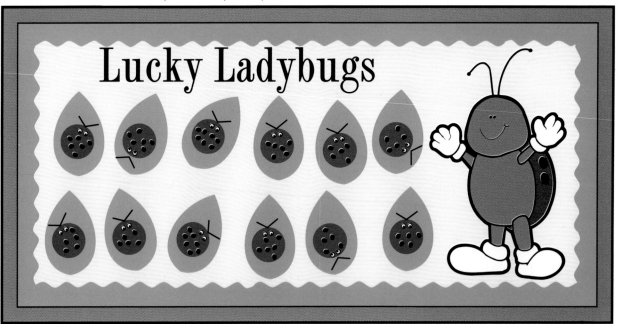

Enlarge, color, and cut out the ladybug character on page 154. Mount it with the title on your board. Have each child trace a leaf pattern and a ladybug pattern onto construction paper and cut them out. Invite the child to make fingerprint spots on her ladybug; then glue on wiggle eyes and pipe-cleaner antennae. Instruct her to glue her ladybug to its leaf. Pin these bugs to the board. You'll be seeing spots!

Peggy Miller—Four- And Five-Year-Olds, Rabbit Hill Nursery School, Springfield, PA

Honor moms with this blue-ribbon display. Duplicate the pattern on page 155 for each child. Have him draw a picture of his mom inside the circle part of the ribbon; then have him color the ribbon blue. Do not write any names on the drawings. Staple these ribbons to a bulletin board. Mothers will get a kick out of trying to guess which ribbon has their picture on it. Send the ribbons home in time for Mother's Day!

Dona Blackmore—Gr. K, Stivers Academy, Livermore, CA

Make a large rocket ship from white paper. Add red and yellow paper streamers to the bottom of the vehicle. Mount the rocket ship on a bulletin board. For each child, duplicate the astronaut pattern on page 153. Have him color, cut out, and attach his astronaut to the board. Below the title, staple a stack of construction-paper squares with individual numerals that can be torn off each day. 5, 4, 3, 2, 1…blast off!

Beth Marie Hall—Gr. K, Bethel Christian Academy, Carlisle, PA

Circulating Circle

Need a tangible way to help youngsters gather during group time? Try this neat way to structure your circle-time area, whether indoors or out! Create a mat by cutting a piece of vinyl flooring into a large circle. Place the mat in the desired location of your group activities—in the classroom, gym, or even the playground; then have students sit around the edges of the mat. After circle time, simply roll up the mat and store it in a closet or corner of the room. This mat is sure to make the rounds!

Diane Shatto—Three- And Four-Year-Olds
St. Elizabeth
Kansas City, MO

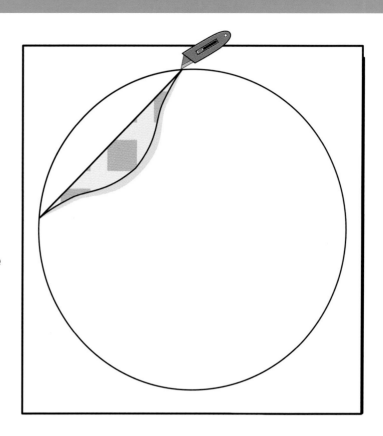

Danny Taylor

September 21, 1996

Circle Time "Feet-ures"

Footprints are the main attraction of this circle-time idea. At the beginning of the school year, invite each child to make a set of footprints on a sheet of tagboard. To do this, have the child step barefoot into a shallow tray of paint, then step carefully onto his sheet of tagboard. After the paint dries, label each set of footprints with the child's name and the date. Laminate the prints for durability. Then tape each child's footprints on the floor in your group-time area. Have each youngster sit on or stand behind his own set of footprints during circle activities throughout the year. At the end of the year, the laminated prints can be removed from the floor, wiped clean, and sent home as keepsakes.

Doris McCauley—Three- And Four-Year-Olds
Rosemont Preschool
Ft. Worth, TX

The Name Game

If your youngsters get confused about where to sit at circle time, spell it out for them! Using colored vinyl tape, spell out each child's name on the floor in your large-group area. Then at circle time, encourage students to find and sit on their names. You might also use the taped names to play letter and name recognition games with the children. After youngsters are able to identify their first names, replace each child's name with his last name or initials. No matter how you use the names on the floor, youngsters will enjoy playing this name game.

Kyle Welby—Gr. K
Epstein Hebrew Academy
St. Louis, MO

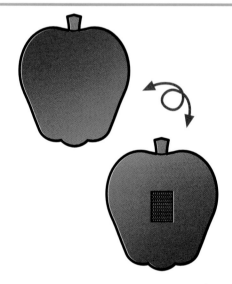

Seasonal Sitters

Keep a seasonal theme flowing through your circle-time gatherings. Cut out a class quantity of construction-paper shapes—such as apples, pumpkins, or snowflakes—to correspond to each season or special occasion of the year. Laminate each set of cutouts or cover each with clear Con-Tact® covering. If your circle-time area is carpeted, attach the hook side of a piece of Velcro® to the back of each cutout; then press the set of cutouts representing the current season onto the carpet. If your classroom floor is not carpeted, simply tape the set onto the floor to form your circle area. Then at group time, invite each youngster to sit on a seasonal shape. These seasonal sitters are sure to keep youngsters in the spirit of the season!

Laura K. Eveland Swanson—Four- And Five-Year-Olds
College Of Lake County Child Care
Grayslake, IL

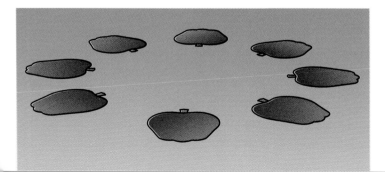

Sign And Share

Looking for a sign that a youngster may have something special to share with the class today? Help him let you know by using this simple sign-up procedure. To prepare, place a dry-erase board near your classroom door. As children enter the room each day, encourage those who wish to share any special news or information with the class to sign their names on the board. During group time, give each child listed on the board the opportunity to share his news with the group; then have him wipe his name off the board. What an easy way to read the signs!

Lisa Kuecker—Gr. K
Adams Elementary
Arkansas City, KS

I have something to share.
Lisa   marvin
Jessie   Jerry

Lip Zippers

If you and your students use the term "Zip your lips" in a playful, positive way, then try teaching this song to help them settle down for circle time.

If You're Ready And You Know It
(sung to the tune of
"If You're Happy And You Know It")

If you're ready and you know it,
Zip your lips!
ZZZiiip!

If you're ready and you know it,
Zip your lips!
ZZZiiip!

If you're ready and you know it,
Then you'll sit right down and show it.

If you're ready and you know it,
Zip your lips!
ZZZiiip!

Jessica Pope
KinderCare Learning Center
Frederick, MD

Praise That Sticks

Praise youngsters in a way that will surely stick with them—by writing compliments on name labels. Print each child's name on a large self-adhesive label. During group time, ask each child's peers to name a few positive things about that child. Write their responses on the child's name label. Then invite that child to wear his label throughout the day. Your proud students will be pleasantly surprised at how praise prompts praise as others admire their good qualities and even add their own positive comments.

Samita Arora—Pre-K
Richmond, IN

Tell, Guess, And Share

Add a different twist to your show-and-tell time with this game. Ask each child to put an item he would like to share with his classmates into a bag, and bring it to school. During group time, invite each child to hold his bagged item as he describes or tells something about it, without revealing the bag's contents. After students have made their guesses about the identity of his item, have him remove it from the bag to show his classmates. With this interesting twist, show-and-tell becomes a fun and interesting game of T.G.S.—Tell, Guess, and Share.

Sarah Simpson—Gr. K
Pinar Elementary
Orlando, FL

Pick A Pal

Here's a "tree-mendous" way to pick a teacher's helper—or pal—for the day. Cut a large tree shape from bulletin-board paper and laminate it for durability. Then cut out a class quantity of construction-paper shapes to coordinate with the current season—such as apples, leaves, or candy canes. Label each cutout with a different child's name. Attach the tree to a wall at a child's eye level. Tape each cutout onto the tree. Each day during circle time, pick a teacher's pal by selecting a name off the tree. Invite the special helper to take the cutout home to let his family know about his special job. Continue choosing a new pal each day until each child has had a turn. Then create a new set of cutouts and begin again.

Adapted from an idea by Jan Steffenauer—Three- And Four-Year-Olds
Lutz Preschool
Danville, PA

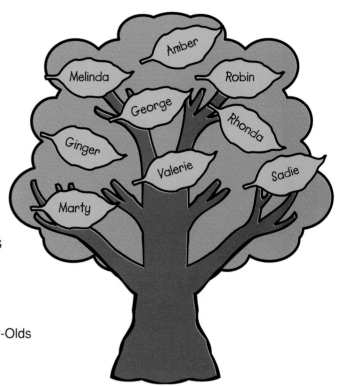

A Model Weather Reporter

Employ your circle-time weather reporter to model appropriate attire for the day's weather with this activity. Place a basket of items to represent different kinds of weather wear—such as jackets, mittens, T-shirts, raincoats, shorts, and sunglasses—near your group-time area. Each day during circle time, invite the class weather reporter to select from the basket several articles appropriate for that day's weather. Ask the child to put on the articles (or to clip them on over his clothing with spring-type clothespins), then to give the weather report. Whether bold or shy, each youngster will enjoy taking his turn as the model weather reporter.

Cindy Magrath—Preschool
Lovell Weekday Ministry
Conway, SC

Person To Person

Promote body awareness and social skills with this circle-time game. During group time, divide youngsters into pairs. Have each student in a pair sit on the floor facing her partner. To play, call out the name of a body part—such as knee, shoulder, or heel. Each partner will touch that part of her body to the same body part on her partner. After calling out several different body parts for the partners to touch together, call out, "Person To Person!" On this signal, each student will leave her partner and find another child to become her new partner. After the new student pairs have been formed, continue the game in the same fashion. Getting to know each other person to person is a fun way to make friends.

Patricia McIntyre—Gr. K
Beechwood On The Bay
Quincy, MA

Heart Sharing

"Share my heart!" will be the call coming from youngsters in this modified game of musical chairs. To prepare, cut out a large construction-paper heart for each child. Laminate the cutouts for durability. Then randomly place the cutouts on the floor. To play, encourage students to walk around the hearts while you play some lively music. Then stop the music and have all the students find a heart to stand on. Before playing the music again, remove one of the hearts. The next time the music stops, a child must share his heart with another child. Continue in this manner, removing a heart each round, until several children must share each heart. This "heart-y" game is a wonderful way for youngsters to form some heartfelt friendships!

Gina Mahony
Children's Preschool Workshop
Barrington, IL

Pick A Poem

Use a class book to encourage youngsters to recite and appreciate poetry. Throughout the year, make copies of age-appropriate poems from a variety of sources—such as children's poetry books, magazines, or other literature. If desired, add a corresponding illustration or photograph to each poetry page for easy identification. Place each page into a separate sheet protector; then put the pages in a binder. Write "Our Book Of Poetry" on the front cover of the binder. Then, during circle time, have a volunteer select a poem from the book to be read to the class. Before long, youngsters will discover their favorite poems and will join in choral recitations of the familiar ones. How glorious are the voices of such young poetry enthusiasts!

Sr. Mary Bezold—Montessori
St. Camillus Academy
Corbin, KY

Our Book Of Poetry

Look Through A Book
I look through a book,
And what do I see?
I see words
Written so carefully.

What Is The Season?

Reinforce the names and appropriate dress for the different seasons with this activity. Put a variety of clothes and accessories representing the four seasons into a basket. For example, you might include a coat, swimsuit, scarf, umbrella, pair of mittens, and shorts in the basket. During group time, whisper the name of a season into a volunteer's ear; then encourage him to select and put on a few articles from the basket appropriate for that season. Have the child name some familiar activities or special days associated with that season. Then ask his classmates to try to guess the name of the season. Look at the clothing. Listen to the clues. Do you know what the season is?

Cindy Magrath—Preschool
Lovell Weekday Ministry
Conway, SC

Ready, Set, Pose!

Youngsters will stick with this fun imitation game for a long time! To prepare, draw a different stick figure on each of several sheets of construction paper—each modeling a different pose. Laminate the pages, if desired; then bind them together with metal rings. During circle time, hold up a stick-figure picture so that all the students can see it. Ask the children to imitate the position of the stick figure. Then flip the book to a different page, and repeat the process. Youngsters will demonstrate a lot of "stick-to-it-tiveness" as they figure out the poses to imitate!

Sr. Mary Bezold—Montessori
St. Camillus Academy
Corbin, KY

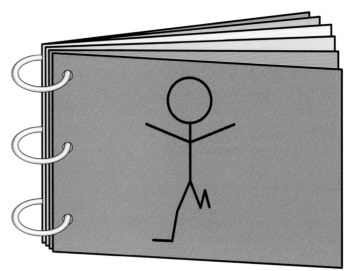

Quietly, quietly, one and all. This is how we walk in the ___.

A story about a giant or a fairy can be found in the school's ___.

Bear Hunt

Lead youngsters on a bear hunt with a honey of a twist. Prior to group time, program a set of construction-paper, bear pawprints with clues so that the clue on one print will lead to the next print. Place the pawprints in sequence around the classroom and school, with the last print leading to the bear cave—the cafeteria, kitchen or snack area. Wear a safari hat and jacket and invite youngsters to go on a bear hunt with you. Lead students from one clue to the next, encouraging them to help figure out the bear's path. When the class reaches the bear's cave, only to find the bear missing, look around and "suddenly" find a treat left behind by the bear—biscuits and honey! Invite youngsters to enter the cave and partake of the beast's kindly offering.

Rhonda Lehmann—Gr. K
Morningside Elementary
Great Falls, MT

Oh, What A Tangled Web...

This weaving idea will add a fun touch to your art center at Halloween or during a unit on spiders. Prepare a class supply of paper plates by punching holes around the rims. Prepare laces by cutting long lengths of black yarn. Tie a large knot in one end of each yarn length; then dip the opposite end into glue and allow it to harden. Place the plates and laces in your art center. Encourage each child to randomly lace a length of yarn in and out of a plate's holes to create a tangled spiderweb. If desired, provide plastic spiders for youngsters to glue to their finished webs.

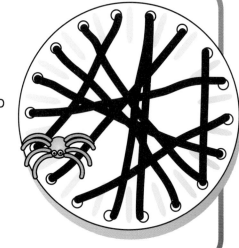

Debbie Quigley—Parent Education
Sweetwater Adult School
National City, CA

Cutting Table

Encourage youngsters to practice scissor skills with this fun center. Check your local craft store or catalogs to find safety scissors with various cutting edges. Provide a wide variety of paper colors and textures, too. Then invite children to come to the table to snip and clip to their heart's content! If desired, trace lines and shapes onto paper for those students who need specific practice with cutting corners or curves.

Amy Provencio—Four-Year-Olds
Merry Moppet Pre-School
Belmont, CA

Fine-Motor Fun

You'll find it's easy to squeeze in some fine-motor skills with this center activity! Prepare a tray with a sponge, a small bottle filled with colored water, an eyedropper, and a plastic soap dish with a suction-cup bottom. (Turn the soap dish upside down so the suction cups are on top.) Demonstrate for students how to fill the eyedropper with colored water, then gently squeeze it to fill each suction cup with a large bead of water. Have students use the sponge for spills and to soak up the water from the suction cups when they are finished.

Sharon Washer—Pre-K
Bolivar-Richburg Preschool
Bolivar, NY

Sand-Table Treasures

Add some excitement to your sand table! Purchase a few packages of metallic confetti from a craft store or a party-supply store. Look for holiday or seasonal shapes that will tie into your themes. Add the confetti to your sand table; then watch youngsters' faces light up when they discover the hidden treasure!

Linda Bille—Three- And Four-Year-Olds
Riviera United Methodist Preschool
Redondo Beach, CA

Less Mess

Consider using an empty sensory table for messy art activities, such as splatter painting or projects involving colored sand. The deep walls of the table will help keep messy materials off carpets and clothing.

Squirrels At The Sensory Center

Your little ones will go nuts over this fun fall activity! Fill your sensory table with crisp autumn leaves. (Use silk leaves from a craft store if the climate in your area doesn't produce fall leaves.) Add a large number of acorns you've gathered or any nuts with shells from the grocery store. Invite small groups of youngsters to role-play squirrels and search for the nuts hidden among the leaves. Have each group compare which squirrel found the most, the fewest, or the same number of nuts.

Adapted from an idea by
Esther Kohn—Four- And Five-Year-Olds
Yeshiva Headstart
Brooklyn, NY

85

Tubes To Tunnels

If your youngsters enjoy using toy cars in your block center, add to the fun by converting cardboard tubes into tunnels. Ask parents to send in empty cardboard tubes from paper towels or gift wrap. Use single tubes as short tunnels or insert the end of one tube into another to create a longer tunnel. Bridge-shaped wooden blocks will help hold the tunnels in place. Watch your young engineers plan, build, and problem-solve!

Colleen Keller—Three- And Five-Year-Olds
Clarion-Goldfield Elementary
Clarion, IA

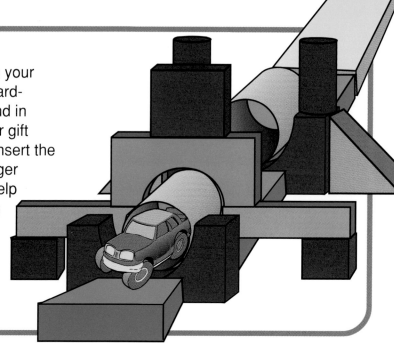

Something Old, Something New

Combat boredom in the block center by rotating sets of building materials with other teachers. Get together with your colleagues and take an inventory of what building toys each teacher has in her classroom—such as Lego® sets, foam blocks, cardboard brick blocks, Lincoln Logs®, etc. Have each teacher keep a basic set—such as wooden blocks—but periodically switch some of the other materials. Children and teachers alike will enjoy the variety!

Thematic Play

Add a thematic touch to your block center. Each time you begin a new theme, look for a related manipulative to place in your block center to spark children's imaginations. Youngsters will enjoy creating mountains and valleys for plastic dinosaurs, building barns for farm-animal figures, or constructing a fishing dock near a paper pond filled with fish counters.

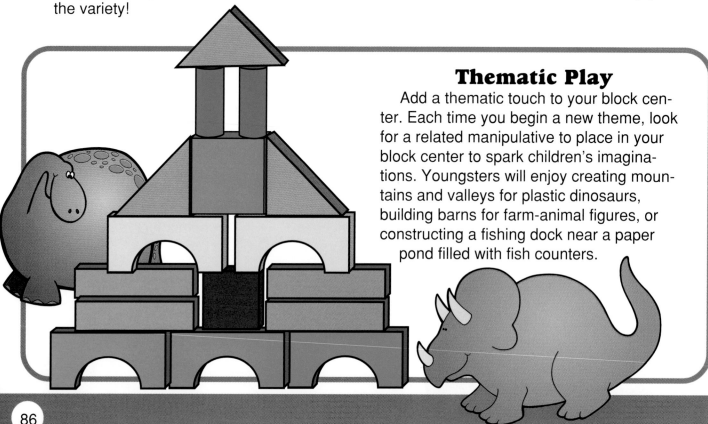

"Brace-let" Yourself For Math Fun!

Bracelets make the perfect accessories for your math center! Gather a supply of inexpensive, colored plastic bracelets. Ask a student volunteer to be your helper as you trace the child's hand and forearm onto several sheets of tagboard. On each tagboard card, draw colored lines that correspond to the colors in your bracelet collection. Place the cards and plastic bracelets in your math area.

To use the center, a child chooses a card, looks at the pattern of bracelet colors, then places the real bracelets on his arm to match the card.

Gina Mello—Pre-K
South Winneshiek Elementary
Ossian, IA

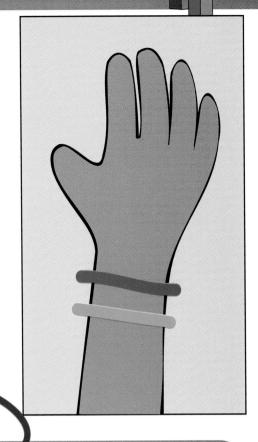

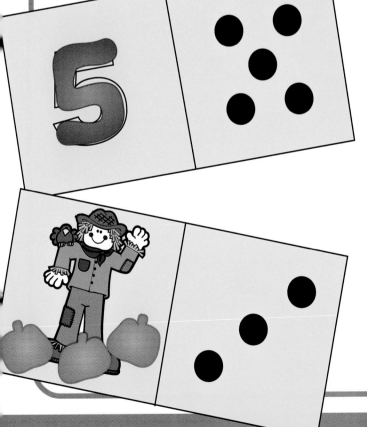

Roll Out The Numbers

Add play dough to your math center and help mold your youngsters' skills with numeral formation and creating sets. Draw large outline numerals on sheets of tagboard; then program each card with a matching set of dots. Laminate the cards for durability. As each child visits the center, invite her to roll some play dough into a long snake, then fit it into the numeral outline on a card. Provide counters or cookie cutters in thematic or seasonal shapes and invite students to create sets to match each numeral they form.

For additional practice with sets, create cards with seasonal pictures and numerals. Invite students to add a corresponding number of play-dough shapes (either molded free-form or cut with cookie cutters) to each seasonal picture.

Jo-Ann Lord—Gr. K
Freetown Elementary School
E. Freetown, MA

Pumpkin Patch

Transform your dramatic-play area into a pumpkin patch for the fall season. Shred brown paper grocery bags and scatter the pieces on the floor to represent hay. Ask parents to send in pumpkins in a variety of sizes and shapes, as well as a few bathroom scales. Provide a toy cash register and play money. Ask youngsters to help you create a banner with the name of your pumpkin patch. When everything is assembled, invite little ones to visit the center to shop for the perfect pumpkin!

Jessica Pope—Two-Year-Olds
Kindercare Learning Center
Germantown, MD

Pope's Pumpkin Patch

Fun With Frosty

Students can dress as one of their favorite cool characters—Frosty The Snowman™— when you add a few props to your dramatic-play area. Gather together a man's black hat, a scarf, a broom, and a child's pair of boots. To make a carrot nose, cut a semicircle from orange construction paper and laminate it for durability. Roll the paper into a cone shape and staple it in place. Then punch a hole in each side of the cone and add an elastic band. Now your Frosty costume is complete!

Joan Banker—Three- And Four-Year-Olds
St. Mary's Child Development Center
Garner, NC

Indoor/Outdoor Dramatic-Play Center

Expand your dramatic-play area by adding an outdoor setting to the traditional kitchen arrangement. To define the outdoor area, purchase a section of lattice from your local home-improvement store. Cut the lattice into two pieces and paint it white, if desired. Arrange the two pieces to form a corner of the dramatic-play "yard." Then add props such as a child's picnic table, some lawn or patio chairs, a mailbox, and a clothesline and clothespins. Create a garden by setting a large plastic tub on the floor. Add florists' foam, plastic or silk flowers, a watering can, gardening gloves, and toy gardening tools. If desired, hang construction-paper cutouts of birds, clouds, and a sun from the ceiling over the outdoor area. A construction-paper tree on a wall will also add to the outdoor feeling.

Add a few touches to this outdoor area as the seasons change. In autumn, sprinkle silk leaves in fall colors on the floor. Add a plastic rake. Place some small pumpkins in the garden, too. For winter, hang paper snowflakes from the ceiling and add cotton balls on the floor and in the tree to represent snow. Put out a plastic snow shovel and a child's sled, hang a string of Christmas lights on the lattice, or place silk poinsettias in the garden. In spring or summer, add a toy lawn mower, a child's swimming pool, or even a lemonade stand! The possibilities for indoor/outdoor pretending are endless!

Karen Eiben—Three-Year-Olds
The Kids' Place
LaSalle, IL

Amy Gray—Pre-K
Peru Catholic
Peru, IL

Lots Of Lotto

Here's a versatile way to make a reusable lotto game. Visit a paper-products store and purchase several of the clear, nine-pocket sheets used to hold baseball cards. For each lotto game, create gameboards by cutting index cards to fit the slots in each sheet. Then make a corresponding set of cover cards (enough to cover all the spaces on all the gameboards). Adapt the game to any theme or skill you want to reinforce. For example, use colored sticky dots to program the cards for a color-matching lotto game. Or label the cards on the sheets with lowercase letters and the cover cards with upper-case letters. Store each set of lotto cards in a separate envelope. Invite small groups of students to play lotto, and periodically change the type of lotto game available in the center.

Deborah Eassa—Three- And Four-Year-Olds
St. Ann's School
Syracuse, NY

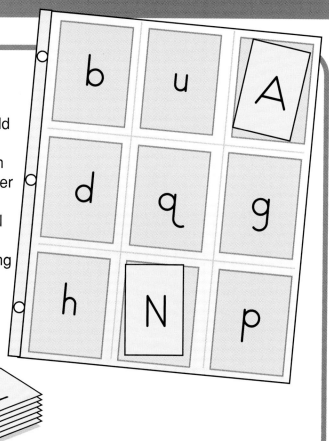

Bug Safari

Add this trail game to your games center during a study of insects. Trace a path similar to the one shown on a sheet of poster board. In each space on the path, affix either a colored sticky dot or an insect sticker. Make corresponding cards with colored sticky dots and insect stickers. If desired, decorate around the path with drawings or clip art. Provide plastic insects to use as game markers. Then invite students to play the game, following rules similar to those for Candyland®. The first player to reach the Bug Jar is the winner!

Cheryl B. Cicioni—Three-, Four-, And Five-Year-Olds
Kindernook Preschool
Lancaster, PA

Mixing Magic

Young children are always fascinated with the magic of color mixing. Give them an opportunity to try it at your science center. Provide a few clear, empty containers; several eyedroppers; and three containers of colored water—one each of red, yellow, and blue. Then encourage youngsters who visit the center to experiment with mixing drops of colored water to create new shades.

Sharon W. Caniglia—Three- And Four-Year-Olds
First Baptist Preschool and Kindergarten of St. Charles
Waldorf, MD

The "Sense-ational" Sea

During a study of the ocean or the beach, create a display table featuring theme-related items. Cover a long table with a colorful beach towel and add items such as sand, a bottle of tanning lotion, pairs of sunglasses, a pail and shovel, a container of fish-shaped crackers, various shells, a cassette recording of ocean sounds, and some ocean-themed books. Encourage students to use all five senses to explore the items in this discovery center.

Sandy O'Connell—Gr. K
M. M. Pierce
Remington, VA

 **Centers**

Write-On Picture Frames

An inexpensive, plastic picture frame can turn a reproducible maze or tracing practice sheet into a reusable activity. Simply insert the reproducible page into the frame and provide wipe-off markers. One student can complete the task on the page, then wipe it clean for another child to use. Use this method to help youngsters practice name writing, as well. Print each child's name on a separate 3" x 5" card and insert each card into a 3" x 5" frame. The frames make wonderful, sturdy name-plates for the table, and youngsters can prac-tice tracing the letters in their names with wipe-off markers.

Judy Knapp—Kindergarten
Wilcox Elementary
Twinsburg, OH

Wipe-Off Book

Here's another idea for making activity sheets reusable. Place them in page-sized, clear protective pockets. Then place all the protective pockets in a three-ring binder. Clip a hole-punched, zippered pencil case into the binder, as well. Place wipe-off markers and crayons in the pencil case. Add the binder to your writing center. A youngster can use the wipe-off markers or crayons to complete the activity pages of his choice, then wipe the protective covers clean for another child to use. Change the activity pages in the binder to keep interest high and help students prac-tice new skills.

Sue DeMoss—Three-, Four-, And Five-Year-Olds
Maquoketa II Headstart
Maquoketa, IA

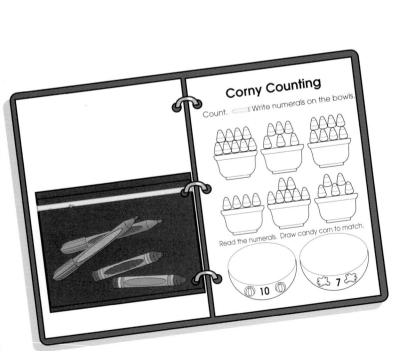

Alphabet Soup

What's cooking in your writing center? How about some alphabet soup? Empty two or three boxes of uncooked alphabet noodles into a large pot. Provide a small ladle and invite each visitor to the center to scoop a serving of noodles into a paper or plastic bowl. Depending on your students' abilities, encourage them to find matching letters, find all the letters of the alphabet and place them in order, spell their names, or spell words from a word list. Mmm…mmm…good practice!

Patricia McIntyre—Gr. K
Beechwood On The Bay
Quincy, MA

Writing-Center Pictures

Scan the coupon section of your Sunday paper to find colorful pictures to use in your writing center. This section usually contains many seasonal pictures and other high-interest pictures for young children. Encourage youngsters to use the pictures as story starters; labels for word lists; or illustrations for cards, postcards, or stories.

Cathy Armstrong—Gr. K
Bain Elementary School
Charlotte, NC

Alphabet Tubs

Tiny treasures will make beginning-sounds practice fun! Check discount or dollar stores to find a collection of little toys and objects representing the beginning sounds for each letter of the alphabet. Store them in a large plastic tub with a snap-on lid. Make sorting tubs by collecting 26 margarine tubs with plastic lids. Cover the top of each lid with Con-Tact® paper; then label each tub with a different letter (using either a permanent marker or vinyl stick-on letters). Invite students to sort the objects into the individual letter tubs. It's as easy as A-B-C!

Tricia Draper—Gr. K
Millarville Community School
Turner Valley, Alberta

Centers

A Seasonal Center

Youngsters will flip over this fun center idea! Designate a corner of your room as a seasonal center. Change the center activities placed there with each new season, holiday, or theme. Include related puzzles, games, craft ideas, books, math manipulatives, etc.

To make this center a surefire hit, decorate the entrance to the center so that it corresponds to the season or theme. Find a large box to fit across the entrance to the center. From both sides of the box, cut a doorway large enough for children to crawl through or duck into. Then use bulletin-board paper, a few craft materials, and your imagination to transform the box into an appealing entryway to the center. Try a haunted house at Halloween, an igloo in winter, or a rainbow for spring. How about a giant apple for the beginning of the school year or a log cabin at Thanksgiving? The possibilities are endless!

Vicki Wright—Gr. K
Mooreland Grade School
Mooreland, OK

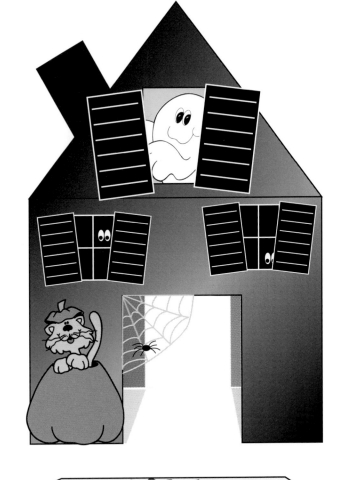

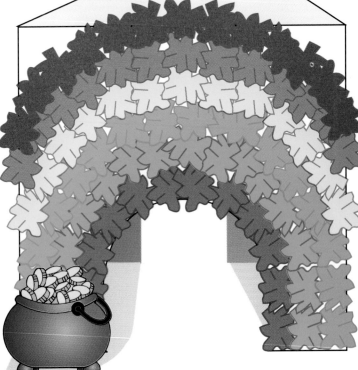

Rain-Forest Reading

Give your reading area the atmosphere of a jungle during a study of the rain forest. Hang loops of twisted, green crepe paper from the ceiling. Have students cut leaves from green construction paper to add to the crepe-paper vines. Cover some wooden blocks with brown bulletin-board paper. Glue Easter grass to one side of each block; then arrange the blocks to form the banks of a blue, bulletin-board-paper river. Ask children to color and cut out pictures of rain-forest animals—such as monkeys, butterflies, turtles, and lizards, to add to the riverbank and the vines. Display books about the rain forest and its inhabitants; then invite youngsters to trek through the jungle to find a good book!

Sandra O'Connell—Gr. K
M. M. Pierce
Remington, VA

Books In The Bathtub

Youngsters will bubble over with excitement when you add a pretend bathtub to your reading center! Obtain a large appliance box. Cut off one long side of the box; then paint the box white. Partially fill the box with Styrofoam® packing pieces. Add a vinyl tub pillow and a rubber ducky to complete the effect. Rub-a-dub-dub! Let's read books in the tub!

Reverse Sponge-Painting

Explore a different method of sponge-painting with your youngsters. Have each child fingerpaint on a sheet of paper. Then—instead of dipping the sponge in paint to make a print—have each child press dry sponge shapes onto the wet paint in order to remove the paint from the paper. The resulting prints will absorb a lot of attention!

Paula Nelson—Preschool
Tea Early Childhood
Tea, SD

Jell-O® Smell-O

Make painting a sensory experience as well as a fine-motor activity. Mix different colors of powdered Jell-O® gelatin with water to create watercolors. Invite children to use paintbrushes and the Jell-O® paints to produce imaginative masterpieces that look great and smell great, too! Don't be surprised to see Jell-O® stains on noses. Sniff, sniff!

Kimberly Calhoun—Three-Year-Olds
Tutor Time Learning Center
Cary, NC

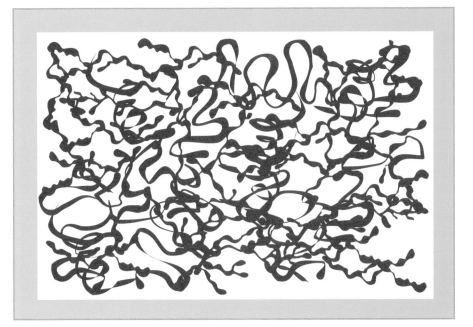

Glue Hues

Provide another unique medium for your little ones to try. Pour some glue into separate cups. Tint the glue in each cup with a different color of food coloring. Direct each child to use cotton swabs to dip and drizzle the colored glues onto her paper. Encourage her to hold and tilt her paper so that the glue can "run" and make more interesting designs. When the glue has dried, display each piece of "glue work" on colored construction paper.

Amy Pierce—Pre-K
Pierce Private Day School, Irving, TX

Colorful Cornmeal Creations

Get down to the nitty-gritty with these painting techniques. Fill several small containers with white cornmeal. Add a different color of food coloring to each container; then mix with a spoon. Let the mixtures dry. Have a child use bottled glue to squirt a design onto his sheet of paper. Then instruct him to sprinkle the colored cornmeal onto the glue.

Or simply add cornmeal to the tempera paints in your painting center. Once children's paintings have dried, they will be able to feel a rough texture. Then display this cornucopia of cornmeal creations!

Melinda Davidson—Preschool
Brockton Early Childhood Program
Brockton, MA

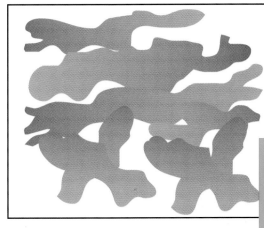

Tissue-Paper Art

A beautiful collage of color will develop when youngsters create with tissue paper and liquid starch. In advance, cut different shades of tissue paper into small squares. For each child, provide a poster-board pattern that correlates with your current unit of study. Pour liquid starch into small containers and provide a paintbrush for each child. Have the child paint her pattern with the starch. Then instruct her to cover the pattern with overlapping tissue squares. Direct her to paint the pattern with a final layer of starch and let it dry. To finish the project, help the child cut off the tissue-paper edges around the pattern.

Mary Hilditch—Three-Year-Olds
Relay Children's Center
Baltimore, MD

Easy Splatter-Paint

Here's a great tip for getting the splatter-paint look without the mess! Cut out a tagboard pattern for each child. Direct him to use a spray bottle to cover his pattern with water. Have him sprinkle powdered tempera paint over the wet pattern. If desired, the pattern can be sprayed with water again. Lay the pattern flat to dry. Little hearts will be pitter-pattering over this fun splattering!

Mary Hilditch—Three-Year-Olds

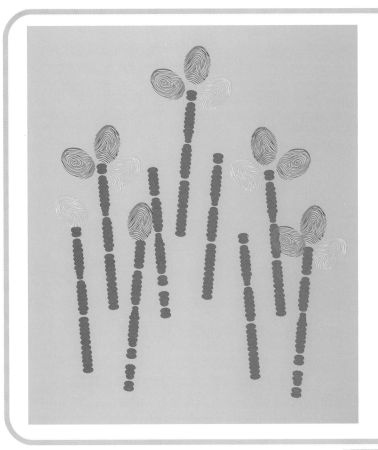

Branches Without Brushes

Encourage youngsters to use pipe cleaners as tools for painting tree or shrubbery branches. Have each child dip a pipe cleaner into a jar of paint; then have her apply the side of the pipe cleaner, with a little pressure, to her paper. Encourage her to decorate the branches with popcorn blossoms, fingerprint leaves, or green tissue-paper leaves depending on the season. Your youngsters will want to branch out and try this crafty technique on other paintings as well!

Marsha Feffer—Four-Year-Olds
Bentley Early Childhood Center
Salem, MA

Boo!

Spook your youngsters with this pop-up ghost picture. For each child, duplicate the pumpkin pattern on page 149 on orange construction paper and the ghost pattern on page 154 on white construction paper. Have each child add features to her ghost with bits of black construction paper. Instruct her to cut out the pumpkin and ghost. Assist the child in cutting off the top of her pumpkin. Have her glue this piece to the top of the ghost's head. Apply glue around the outer sides and bottom of the back of the pumpkin. Have each child glue the resulting pumpkin pocket to a sheet of black construction paper. Once the glue is dry, have her slip the ghost inside her pumpkin. For the ghost to reappear, have the child pull up the stem. Boo!

Sue McClimans—Three-Year-Olds
Edwards School
Davenport, IA

Turkey Talk

Turn old magazines into colorful turkey feathers. Trace a turkey head and circle-shaped body onto brown construction paper for each child. Have the child cut out her patterns and glue them onto another piece of construction paper. Provide old magazines and instruct each child to cut out oval feather shapes from the colorful pages. Encourage her to glue the feathers to her turkey's body and use crayons to add the turkey's legs, eyes, and wattle. These birds will be the talk of the town. Gobble, gobble, gobble!

Carol Corby—Gr. K
St. Aloysius School
Jackson, NJ

Holiday Adornments

Help your little ones make these puzzle frames to adorn Christmas trees or refrigerators during the holidays. Gather a supply of old discarded puzzles and spray-paint the pieces green (for wreaths) or blue (for dreidels). For each child, cut either a circle (wreath) pattern from green poster board or a dreidel pattern from blue poster board. Then gather a photo of each child. If you are making wreaths, cut each picture into a circle, about one inch smaller in diameter than your wreath pattern. If you are making dreidels, trim the photos to fit the center section of your dreidel pattern.

Have each child use tacky glue to attach his school picture to the center of his pattern. Direct the child to glue the colored puzzle pieces to the pattern around his picture, trying not to go over the pattern's edge. Invite him to decorate his wreath with red sequins or his dreidel with blue sequins. Once the glue is dry, add a loop of yarn through a hole punched in the top of the frame or attach a piece of magnetic tape to the back. Happy Holidays!

Sandra Shapiro—Four-Year-Olds
The Learning Tree, Fort Myers, FL

Oh Christmas Tree!

Let the sun shine in through these cellophane celebrations. To prepare, duplicate two copies of the Christmas tree pattern on page 156 on green construction paper for each child. Also obtain several sheets of cellophane in different colors, and cut each sheet into small squares. Have each child stack her two patterns together and cut out the pattern through both thicknesses of paper. Assist each child in cutting several holes in the tree pattern, again through both thicknesses of paper. Then have her separate the trees and glue squares of cellophane to cover the holes of one tree. Have her apply glue to the other tree cutout, then place that tree on top of the first so that the cellophane is sandwiched between the two. When the glue has dried, hang the trees near a light source. It will be hard to determine which are glowing more, the trees or your youngsters' faces!

Carol Corby—Gr. K
St. Aloysius School, Jackson, NJ

Light Up The Holidays

Promote the spirit of giving by helping your students make these precious candleholders to give to loved ones. Each child will need a clean baby-food jar (with the label removed), a votive candle, colored tissue paper, liquid starch, and a paintbrush. Print each child's name on the bottom of a different jar with a permanent marker. Have the children tear the tissue paper into small thumbprint-size pieces. To make a holder, instruct each child to place a piece of paper on his jar and paint over it with starch. Have him do this again and again, overlapping the pieces of paper and covering the entire outside of the jar. Once the jar is covered with paper, direct the child to apply one more layer of starch. When the jar is dry, invite him to place the votive candle inside. Someone is going to feel very loved when given this special "stained glass" gift!

Laurie Birt—Gr. K, Belinder School, Prairie Village, KS

A Tisket, A Tasket ...

... an ornament from a basket? Sure! For each child, cut the bottom from a plastic berry basket. Pour some glue and glitter in separate plates or pie tins. Have each child dip his basket bottom in the glue, then in the glitter. When that side of the basket bottom is dry, have him dip the other side. Tie a piece of string around one prong of the dried ornament for hanging. As a variation, use only silver glitter for dipping and the basket bottoms will resemble glistening snowflakes. Either way, your youngsters will enjoy making these glitzy decorations!

Trish Davis—Gr. K, Poplarville Lower Elementary
Poplarville, MS

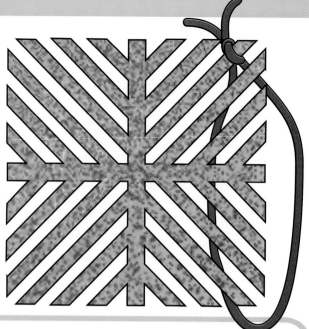

Feeding Frenzy

Welcome winter by having your little ones make these cute bird-feeder replicas. Assist them in following the steps below; then listen to the chirps of delight!

Materials Needed (per child):
Four 1" x 5" rectangles of black construction paper
One 1" x 8" rectangle of black construction paper
One 12" x 18" sheet of white construction paper
One 4 1/2" square of colored plastic wrap
One trapezoid (bottom side measuring 8") cut from
    colored construction paper
Birdseed
Two colored craft feathers
Two small wiggle eyes
Construction-paper scraps
Glue
Crayons

Instructions:
1. Glue the four rectangles together to make a square.
2. Glue the long rectangle post to the bottom of the square.
3. Place the resulting feeder on the white paper and trace the inside of the square onto the white paper.
4. Glue birdseed inside the traced square.
5. Glue the plastic-wrap square to the back of the feeder.
6. Glue the feeder to the white paper so that the plastic wrap is on top of the birdseed.
7. Glue the trapezoid roof to the white paper at the top of the feeder.
8. Use scraps to make two bird bodies; then glue the birds to the white paper.
9. Decorate the birds by gluing on the eyes and feathers.
10. Use a crayon to draw snow.

Sandra O'Connell—Gr. K, M. M. Pierce, Remington, VA

Valentine Mail!

Reinforce community-helper awareness by setting up mailboxes for valentine delivery. Obtain a classroom supply of the plastic boxes from Maxwell House® coffee filter packs. Wrap a 5 1/2" x 18" strip of white or pink construction paper around each box and glue it in place. Glue a flag shape cut from red construction paper near the opening of each box. Then invite each child to use stickers, markers, or glitter pens to decorate his box. Attach a heart cutout with his name or picture to the inside of the lid. Line up the finished boxes on a counter top or bookshelf within students' reach. Keep the lids open for little mail carriers to identify the recipients of their special valentines. Special delivery!

Joan Banker—Four-Year-Olds
St. Mary's Child Development Center
Garner, NC

Tulip Tubes

Warm up your classroom with these colorful tulips. To prepare, collect an assortment of paper-towel and toilet-tissue tubes. Cut two half-inch slits in one end of each tube. Cut several tulip patterns from tagboard. Give each child an old file folder. Have her trace the tulip pattern onto the folder, then paint the tulip red, pink, yellow, or purple. Ask her to choose a tube and paint it green. When the paint is dry, have the child cut out the tulip and insert it into the slits on the tube. Encourage her to add green construction-paper leaves to the stem. After the tulips have brightened a windowsill for a while, let each child pick her flower from the garden to enjoy at home.

Lynne Bordeaux—Preschool
Miss Tanya's Nursery School
Westboro, MA

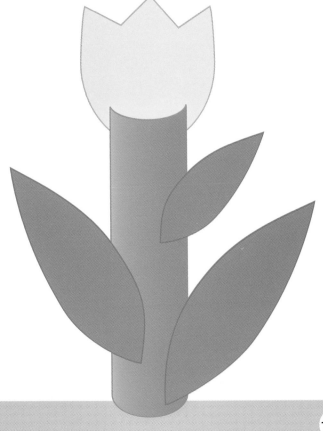

Baby-Food Bunny

Hop into the spring season with bunnies made from baby-food jars. To make one, cut ears from white and pink construction paper. Glue the ears together (pink on top of white); then glue them to the lid of a clean baby-food jar. Glue cotton balls to cover the entire jar and lid. Cut eyes from black construction paper and a nose from pink paper. Glue or tape a few sprigs of broom straw to the back of the nose cutout. Glue the eyes, nose, and whiskers to the cotton. Here comes Peter Cottontail!

Carol Corby—Gr. K
St. Aloysius School
Jackson, NJ

Bubbly Eggs

Here's a tip for creating unique patterns and colors on egg-shaped cutouts. Mix together tempera paint, water, and two tablespoons of dishwashing detergent in a pie tin. Invite each child to use a separate straw to blow into the mixture to create loads of bubbles. Then have her place a piece of construction paper on top of the bubbles. Instruct her to lift the paper and lay it flat to dry. Once it is dry, have her trace an egg pattern onto her painting and cut it out. Display these bubbly eggs in a paper basket cutout or around an Easter bulletin board. Hippity, hoppity, Easter's on its way!

Kimberly Calhoun—Three-Year-Olds
Tutor Time Learning Center
Cary, NC

...she buys me clothes.

...she cooks real good.

...she likes to play with me.

...she is nice.

I love my mommy because...

Mum's Day

Help your children surprise their mommies on Mother's Day with these personalized flowers. To begin, cut a tagboard circle for each child. Make a few petal patterns from tagboard, too.

Have each child use the patterns to trace and cut out four petals from colored construction paper. Have him glue the petals to the tagboard circle to create a flower. While the glue is drying, have him paint a craft stick with green tempera paint. Then invite him to decorate the flower's center to resemble his mother, adding yarn hair if desired. Glue the flower to the craft-stick stem. On each petal, write the child's dictation telling one reason he loves his mother. Place a lump of clay into a small flower-pot for each child; then have him stick the stem of his flower into the clay. Wrap each pot with a square of colorful cellophane wrap, tucking the excess wrap inside the pot. Attach a paper heart cutout labeled with "I love my mommy because …" to the front of each flowerpot. Send the flowers home on the last school day before Mother's Day.

Tracy Tavernese—Four-Year-Olds
Holy Child School, Old Westbury, NY

Creative Corsage

Celebrate Mother's Day by having your children make these "hand-some" corsages for their moms. Help each child trace around her hands on colored paper, then cut on the out-lines. Overlap the palms, then staple the hand cutouts together. Show the child how to roll the fingers of the cutouts around a pencil so that they resemble flower petals. Staple the hand cutouts to the center of a six-inch doily. Cover the staple with a ribbon bow. Tape a safety pin to the back of the doily. Encourage your little ones to give their moms a helping hand along with this corsage on her special day!

Lori Lafratta—Four- And Five-Year-Olds
Garden Gate Preschool
West Seneca, NY

Spring Blossoms

Little ones can grow lots of these unique flowers with no seeds or dirt! In advance, glue a block of Styrofoam® to the inside bottom of a cup or small plastic flowerpot. Each child will need three pipe cleaners, three copies of the flower pattern on page 154, and green crepe-paper scraps. She will also need access to paint, sponges, scissors, and plastic grass.

To make a blossom bunch, have the child sponge-paint her flower patterns with her choice of colors. Once the paint is dry, instruct her to cut out each flower along the outside circle, then snip the inside dotted lines in order to separate the petals. If desired the petals can be curled. Have the child poke a different pipe cleaner through the middle of each flower and slide on crepe-paper leaves. Direct her to stick each pipe cleaner into the block of Styrofoam®. To complete the potted look, have her fill the rest of the container with plastic grass. No watering required!

Cheryl B. Cicioni—Three-, Four-, And Five-Year-Olds
Kindernook Preschool, Lancaster, PA

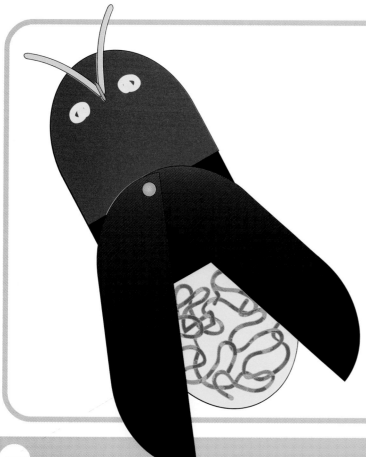

Flickering Firefly

Fireflies are fun to catch, but even more fun to make. Using the patterns on page 157, make two black ovals (one of each size), one red head, and one yellow tail for each child. Have each child cut out his patterns. Help him cut the smaller black oval in half lengthwise to make two wings. Ask the child to glue the red head to one end of the big black oval and the yellow tail to the other end. Provide chalk, glue, and gold glitter for the child to draw the eyes and decorate the tail as shown. Staple a short piece of yellow pipe cleaner to the head for antennae. Attach the wings just below the head with a brad. These illuminating insects will leave lots of little faces all aglow!

Peggy Miller—Four- And Five-Year-Olds
Rabbit Hill Nursery School, Springfield, PA

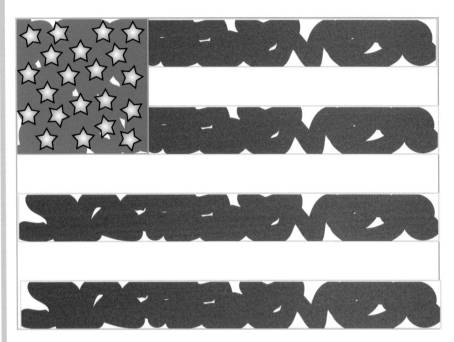

Fingerpainted Flag

Encourage little fingers to get moving in order to create this fabulous flag. Have each child fingerpaint one sheet of paper red and one sheet of paper blue. When dry, instruct her to cut the red paper into strips, then glue the strips across a rectangular sheet of white paper. Help the child cut the blue fingerpainted paper into a square to fit the upper left-hand corner of the white paper. Have the child glue this square to the paper. Provide white star cutouts or silver self-adhesive stars for the child to stick to the blue square. It's a grand old flag!

Roxeanne M. Lansing
Rainbow Room Family Day Care
Ballston Spa, NY

Fourth Of July Fun

Celebrate the Fourth with this neat fireworks display. Bring in several stems of Queen Anne's lace (or similar flowering plant). Using several different colors of paint, provide a dish of paint for each stem. Give each child a sheet of black paper. Invite him to dip the flowers into the paints, and then press them flat onto his paper. Then have him sprinkle glitter onto the wet paint. Display all of the prints together for a night sky filled with fabulous fireworks fun!

Christine Dise—Four-Year-Olds
Pottstown YMCA, Pottstown, PA

Graham Ghosts

Here's a supersimple treat to make near Halloween. Have each child use a craft stick or a plastic knife to spread a spoonful of cream cheese on a graham cracker. Invite him to add raisin eyes and a raisin mouth to the resulting ghost shape. "Boo-tiful!"

Gloria Barrow—Gr. K, Dundee Elementary, Dundee, FL

Tortilla Snowflakes

Bring the snow indoors on a winter day with this fun-to-make snack. Have each child gently fold a flour tortilla in half two times, to make a wedge shape. Show him how to use *clean* safety scissors to cut sections out of the tortilla, just as he would to make a paper snowflake. Heat two tablespoons of oil in an electric frying pan. Cook each child's unfolded tortilla for about 15 seconds on each side (replenishing the oil as necessary). Drain on a paper towel, then sprinkle with powdered sugar. Now *that's* a cool treat!

Mary Wisniewski—Three-, Four-, And Five-Year-Olds
Twinbrook School
Hoffman Estates, IL

Inside Snowman

Your youngsters can have fun making this snowman without even getting cold! Invite students to help you prepare a box of cake mix according to the package directions. Pour the batter into three round cake pans, using two pans that are identical in size and one that is slightly smaller. Bake according to the package directions; then cool the cake layers. Arrange the layers on a large tray as shown. Spread canned white frosting over the cake layers. Add a miniature carrot for a nose, chocolate kisses for eyes, pretzels for eyebrows, cinnamon candies for a mouth, miniature marshmallows for buttons, and licorice-stick arms to complete this snowman snack.

Brenda P. Purvis—Gr. K
Asheville Christian Academy
Asheville, NC

Bunny Biscuits

"Every-bunny" will love this springtime treat! Give each child a six-inch square of waxed paper, a craft stick, and two rounds from a roll of refrigerated biscuits. Have each youngster use her craft stick to cut one biscuit in half. Have her pinch together the two halves and the circle as shown, to form a bunny face and ears on her waxed paper. Have her add raisins for eyes, half of a maraschino cherry for a nose, and a few slivered almonds for whiskers. Place each child's bunny biscuit on a baking sheet; then bake the biscuits at 375° F for ten minutes. Cool; then serve with jam.

Marybeth Castelluzzo—Four-Year-Olds, St. Clement's School, Chicago, IL

Best Nests

This "tweet" treat will add some cooking fun to a unit about birds. To make snacks for 16 children, melt together a 12-ounce package of chocolate chips and one cup of crunchy peanut butter in an electric frying pan set on low heat. Remove the mixture from the heat. Have student volunteers break apart nine large biscuits from a box of shredded-wheat cereal. Stir the crushed cereal into the chocolate mixture. Have each child mold a spoonful of the cooled mixture into a nest shape; then provide jelly-bean eggs for children to place inside their nests. Place all the nests on a baking sheet and refrigerate for two hours until firm.

Diane Parette—Gr. K, Durham Elementary, Durham, NY

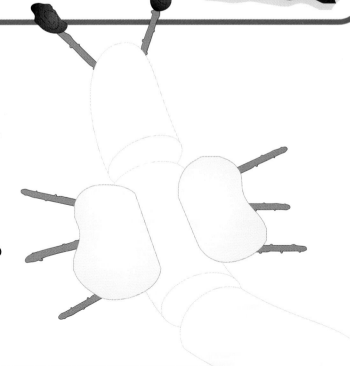

Insects You Can Eat

These edible insects are very educational! Provide each child with a peeled banana and a plastic knife on a paper plate. Show him how to cut the banana into three equal parts to represent the three body parts of an insect. Have each youngster poke six pretzel sticks into the center section of the banana to represent the insect's six legs. Have him insert two more pretzel sticks—topped with raisins—into the top section of the banana to represent antennae. If desired, ask each child to add two potato-chip wings to his insect before eating it up. Yum!

Melinda Davidson—Integrated Special Needs Preschool
Washington, NJ

Banana Boats

Sail into snacktime with these fun treats! In advance prepare a sail for each child by wrapping a short length of masking tape around one end of a toothpick. Trim the masking tape to look like a sail. Provide each youngster with a paper plate, a plastic knife, a peeled banana, and a small cup containing two tablespoons of peanut butter. Have each youngster slice her banana in half lengthwise. Have her spread peanut butter on the flat sides of the banana halves, then put them back together and set the banana on her plate as shown. Encourage each child to stick a sail into the top of her banana boat. Once each youngster has admired her creation, have her remove the toothpick sail and bite into that boat!

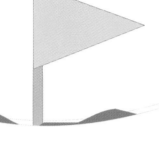

Gloria Barrow—Gr. K
Dundee Elementary
Dundee, FL

Traffic-Light Snack

This simple snack will fit right in with a unit on safety or colors. In advance break whole graham crackers into smaller rectangles and prepare a small plastic bag of M&M's® for each child. Have each child use a craft stick to spread peanut butter on a small graham cracker. Then have her select a red, a yellow, and a green candy from her bag. Have her place the M&M's® atop the peanut butter to resemble the lights on a traffic signal. Invite her to munch her remaining M&M's®, along with her completed snack.

Ann Rochon—Special Needs Preschool, Westerville City Schools, Westerville, OH

Racin' Raisin Cars

Enhance a transportation theme with this race-car recipe. In advance wash a bunch of grapes and several celery stalks. Cut the celery into three-inch sections. Have each youngster use a craft stick to spread cream cheese in the crevice of a celery section. Then insert four toothpicks into each child's celery stalk, as shown. Have each child add four grape wheels and a few raisin passengers to finish his vehicle. On your mark, get set,...eat!

Gloria Barrow—Gr. K

Child-Sized Cheesecakes

Here's a tasty snack for any time! Begin by lining the cups of a muffin tin with foil cupcake liners. Place a vanilla wafer in each liner. To make enough filling for 24 cheesecakes, have youngsters help you mix together four 8-ounce packages cream cheese (softened), two teaspoons vanilla, and one cup sugar until well-blended. Add four eggs and mix well. Pour the mixture over the vanilla wafers, filling each cup three-fourths full. Bake at 325°F for 25 minutes. Cool; then remove the liners from the muffin tin and refrigerate the cheesecakes. Provide fruit, nuts, or jam for children to put on top of their cheesecakes. Delicious!

Diane Parette—Gr. K, Durham Elementary, Durham, NY

Fruit Pizza

Make this sweet treat as a large-group or individual cooking project. For a whole-class pizza, roll out refrigerated sugar-cookie dough into a large circle. Place the circle of dough onto a pizza pan and bake at 350°F until golden brown. Mix together a 16-ounce jar of marshmallow creme and an 8-ounce package of cream cheese. Then have student volunteers spread this mixture over the cooled cookie crust. Add fruit toppings, such as sliced strawberries, banana wheels, kiwi slices, or grape halves. Sprinkle the pizza with shredded coconut before slicing and serving.

To make individual pizzas, slice the cookie dough and place the slices far apart on a cookie sheet. Bake the cookies according to the package directions. Have each child spread a spoonful of the cream-cheese mixture over his cookie and top it with the fruit toppings of his choice.

Diana Long—Three- And Four-Year-Olds
Wesleyan Kiddie College
Bartlesville, OK

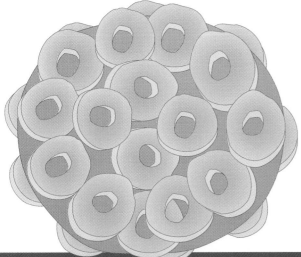

Cheerio® Chews

Little ones can help you make this simple, no-bake treat in the morning, then eat it as an afternoon snack. For each group of eight students, measure and mix together 1/2 cup confectioner's sugar, 1/2 cup light corn syrup, and 1/2 cup peanut butter. Add two cups Cheerios® cereal and stir well. Roll the mixture into balls and place the balls on a baking sheet. Refrigerate for two hours until firm.

Diane Parette—Gr. K

A Very Special Me

Build self-esteem and body awareness when you teach youngsters this rhyme about someone very special—"Me!"

I have hands to clap and wiggle.
I have feet to stomp and jiggle.
With ears that hear and a mouth to sing,
I can do most anything!

Clap hands, then wiggle fingers.
Stomp, then jiggle feet.
Point to ears, then mouth.
Point thumbs at chest with pride.

My eyes can see, my mind pretend.
I have two arms to hug a friend.
With all these things, I'm happy to be
A very, very special me!

Point to eyes, then temples.
Give a pretend hug.
Hold out hands palms up and smile.
Point to self.

Cheryl B. Cicioni—Four-Year-Olds, St. Anne's School At St. John Neumann Church, Lancaster, PA

We Love To Go To Our School

Teach this cute ditty to youngsters to help them express their delight at going to school.

(sung to the tune of "Miss Lucy Had A Baby")

We love to go to our school.
Oh, it is so much fun!
We laugh and play and learn all day,
Until our time is done!

Susan Brown—Gr. K
Southside Elementary
Tuscumbia, AL

Just One Birthday

Use this verse to help little ones learn the parts of their bodies as well as their birthdays. Encourage youngsters to point to their body parts as they recite the rhyme; then ask each child, in turn, to give the date of her birthday at the end of the rhyme.

I have two eyes, two hands, two feet.
But just one nose, one head, one seat.
I have two arms, two legs, two ears.
But just one birthday every year!

Adapted from an idea by Ann Larberg—Three- And Four-Year-Olds
First Presbyterian Day School, DeLand, FL

The Months Of The Year

Use this tune to teach youngsters the names and sequence of the months of the year.

(sung to the tune of "Ten Little Indians")

January, February, March, and April.
May and June, July and August.
September, October, November, December.
Twelve months in a year!

Deborah Well—Gr. K, B. R. Ryall YMCA, Glen Ellyn, IL

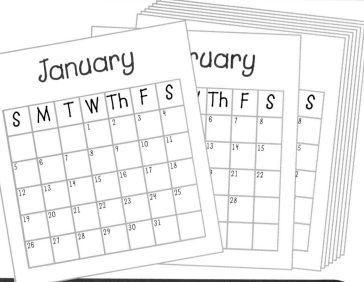

What Is The Weather?

Involve the entire class in participating in the weather report with this rhyme. After the weather reporter checks the weather, ask the class to recite this verse. At the end of the verse, have the weather reporter answer by telling the weather conditions.

Weather reporter,
Can you tell us
What the weather
Is today?

Is it snowy?
Cloudy? Rainy?
Or is it a bright
And sunny day?

Patricia McIntyre—Gr. K, Beechwood On The Bay, Quincy, MA

Time To Put The Toys Away

Make transition time from play to the next activity enjoyable with this song.

(sung to the tune of "Twinkle, Twinkle, Little Star")

Now it's time to stop our play.
Please put all the toys away.
Please be quick and please be neat.
Help until the job's complete.
Now it's time to stop our play.
Please put all the toys away.

Sue Trujillo—Three-, Four-, And Five-Year-Olds
Our Lady Of The Lake Preschool
Mahomet, IL

Singing Shapes

Teach youngsters shapes and colors while singing this song. To make flannelboard figures to accompany the song, cut each desired shape from a different color of construction paper. Laminate the shapes; then glue simple facial features onto each shape—such as wiggle eyes, a pom-pom nose, and a pipe-cleaner smile. Attach the hook side of a piece of Velcro® to the back of each shape. Have a volunteer select and place a shape on the flannelboard as youngsters say the rhyme. Then repeat the rhyme, replacing the underlined phrase with words to describe the next shape to be placed on the flannelboard by the next volunteer.

(sung to the tune of "This Old Man")

[Yellow square] is my name.
Won't you come and play this game?
A great big hug and a kiss to you I'll send.
Won't you come and be my friend?

Joan Banker—Four-Year-Olds
St. Mary's Child Development Center
Garner, NC

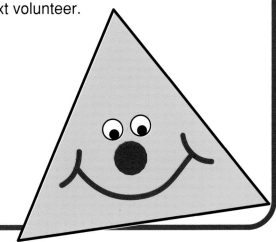

The Lineup Song

Here's a clap-happy way to line up youngsters in an orderly fashion. Sing the song below, using the name of a child in your class. Clap your hands together twice at the end of the first, second, and last lines, as indicated. Each time you repeat the song, use a different child's name until every child is in line. Invite youngsters to join in the singing and clapping as you name each child, in turn, to take her place in line.

*(sung to the tune of
"If You're Happy And You Know It")*

If your name is [Melissa], get in line. X X
If your name is [Melissa], get in line. X X
If [Melissa] is your name,
It's your turn to play the game.
If your name is [Melissa], get in line. X X

Melissa L. Olinger—Four-Year-Olds
Little Friends Preschool
Denver, CO

On The Snack Track

Get youngsters on track as they prepare for snacktime with this choo-choo chant. To begin, divide your class into groups of five students; then have each group line up to resemble a line of train cars. Encourage each group to move in place like a train while saying the chant below. When you say the last line of the first verse, have the child in the mentioned position leave the line and sit down for snacktime. In the same fashion repeat the first verse, each time replacing the underlined words with *four* and *fourth, three* and *third,* and *two* and *second,* consecutively. Then have the last child in each group join the others in the snack area as you say the next verse. After all the students are seated for snacktime, sing the last verse of the song; then serve them their snacks. Having a snack attack? Then get on track!

1. [Five] little train cars going down the track.
   The [fifth] car said, "It's time for a snack."
   Clickety, clickety, clickety, clack!

2. One little train car going down the track.
   The little car said, "It's time for a snack."
   Clickety, clickety, clickety, clack!

3. No little train cars going down the track.
   All the cars are ready for a snack.
   Munchity, munchity, munchity, smack!

Marjorie Eisenwine, South St. Marys St. Elementary, St. Marys, PA

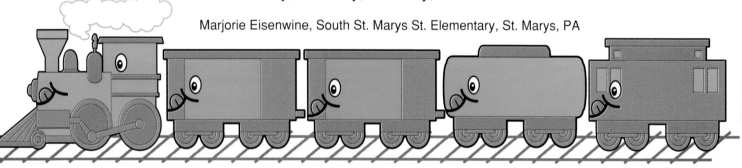

Milk Motivation

Do your youngsters need a little extra encouragement to drink their milk? Try singing this motivational song to get them to partake of this "moo-velous" drink.

Drink Your Milk
(sung to the tune of "Row, Row, Row Your Boat")

Drink, drink, drink your milk.
Drink it every day.
Milk helps your bones and teeth grow strong.
So drink some every day!

Anne Nielson-Poillucci—Three- And Four-Year-Olds, Dove's Nest, Rockland, MA

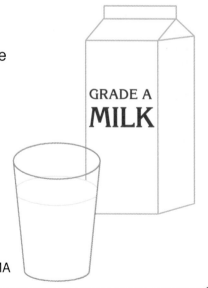

GRADE A
MILK

Scampering Squirrels

Use these scampering squirrels to reinforce counting skills. Duplicate the squirrel patterns on page 148 on brown construction paper. Cut out each pattern; then laminate each cutout for durability. Attach the hook side of a piece of Velcro® to the back of each cutout. Place the cutouts on a flannelboard. Say the rhyme, inviting a different volunteer to remove each squirrel from the board to correspond to the rhyme.

Four baby squirrels in a big oak tree.
One jumped down.
Now there are three.

Three baby squirrels with nothing to do.
One chased its tail.
Now there are two.

Two baby squirrels looking for some fun.
One ran away.
Now there is one.

One baby squirrel, lonely as can be.
Wishing the others
Were back in the tree.

"I'll go get them!" he
    bravely said.
Then he fell down
And bumped his head.

Then mama squirrel called them home to rest.
Four baby squirrels
Scampered to their nest.

Cheryl B. Cicioni—Three-, Four-, And Five-Year-Olds, Kindernook Preschool, Lancaster, PA

The Halloween Scene

Invite youngsters to make a companion book for this counting rhyme. To make a book, have each child sponge-paint the corresponding number of characters mentioned in each line of the rhyme on separate sheets of programmed construction paper. Then sequence the completed pages between two construction-paper covers and title the book "The Halloween Scene." Encourage students to follow along in their books as they recite the rhyme.

One black cat jumping through the air.
Two blue spiders creeping without care.
Three orange jack-o'-lanterns smiling bright.
Four black bats flapping in the night.
Five white ghosts scaring up a scene.
All are wishing you a Happy Halloween!

Kathy Crozier—Gr. K
Greenwood Lake Elementary
Greenwood Lake, NY

Hanukkah Candles

Reinforce basic counting skills with this catchy little tune about the candles in a menorah.

(sung to the tune of "Ten Little Indians")

One little, two little, three little candles.
Four little, five little, six little candles.
Seven little, eight little, nine little candles.
In my Hanukkah menorah!

Bev Finnicum—Three- And Four-Year-Olds
Beth Hillel Nursery School
Bloomfield, CT

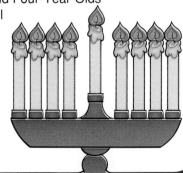

Two Little Leprechauns

Engage little ones in some fun with their imaginations as they say this chant and perform the suggested hand gestures. After saying the rhyme, encourage students to speculate about the mysterious disappearance of these tiny creatures.

(chant to the rhythm of "Three Little Monkeys")

Two small leprechauns, *Hold up two fingers.*
Tiny as can be, *Hold first finger near thumb to indicate small.*
Tipped their hats *Motion as if to tip hat.*
And winked at me. *Point to eye and wink.*

Both were dressed in green *Tug at shirt near shoulders.*
From their heads to their toes. *Point to head, then toes.*
Where are they hiding now? *Hold hands outstretched and shrug shoulders.*
Nobody knows! *Shake head.*

Janet S. Vaughn—Director, First Congregational Church Preschool, LaGrange, IL

Ants, Beware!

Springtime is picnic time! And here's a delightful rhyme youngsters will enjoy reciting, whether on a real or an imaginary picnic.

Little ants go marching
Across my picnic plate.
Little ants, be careful—
That's my lunch you ate!
If you had any manners,
You'd crawl down right away.
And go marching,
 marching,
  marching,
Somewhere else today!

Cheryl Cicioni—Pre-K
St. Anne's Preschool At
 St. John Neumann Church
Lancaster, PA

From Me With Love

Teach youngsters this song to sing to each of their parents on special days, or for any day of the year! Remind children to replace the underlined words with *Dad* and *Daddy* when they sing the song to their fathers.

(sung to the tune of "This Old Man")

I love [Mom]. [Mom] loves me.
We're a loving family.
I have lots of hugs
And kisses to give you.
Oh yes, [Mommy], I love you!

Adapted from an idea by Christine Dise—
 Four-Year-Olds
Pottstown YMCA
Pottstown, PA

Roll A Story

Students will be on a storytelling roll when they use these special dice as story starters. To make a die, cut off the bottoms of two clean half-gallon milk or juice cartons; then fit one inside the other to create a cube. Cover the die with a solid color Con-Tact® covering. Tape photos showing students engaged in actions—such as cutting, sitting, and dancing—on each side of one die. On each side of another die, tape a different picture of a person or an animal. To use, invite a child to roll the dice. Then encourage her to make up a story based on the pictures which appear on the top of each die. For instance, she might roll a dog and the action picture for cutting, then go on to tell a story about a dog that cut out bone-shaped cards for its friends. If desired, write each child's dictated story on a sheet of paper; then have her illustrate her story. Compile the illustrated stories into a book titled "On A Roll."

Diane E. Parette—Gr. K, Durham Elementary, Durham, NY

In The News

Extra! Extra! Read all about it! Youngsters will eagerly read this special newspaper section featuring one of their classmates. Print "Great News About [Child's Name]" in bold letters on the inside of a sheet of newspaper. Each week have a different child create a few illustrations telling about himself. Write his dictation about his illustrations on paper strips; then glue the illustrations and paper strips inside the newspaper section under the title. Fold that section, and nestle it into another section of the newspaper. During group time, ask a child to find the "Great News!" section of the paper. After he locates the special section, read aloud the child-generated news and show the corresponding illustrations to the class. Then invite the featured child to take the special section home to share the news with his family.

Kay Dawson—Gr. K
B. C. Charles Elementary
Newport News, VA

Great News About Daniel
Classifieds

I'm going to be the best firefighter ever!

My dog's name is Bobo. He sleeps in my room.

I like to ride my bike really fast!

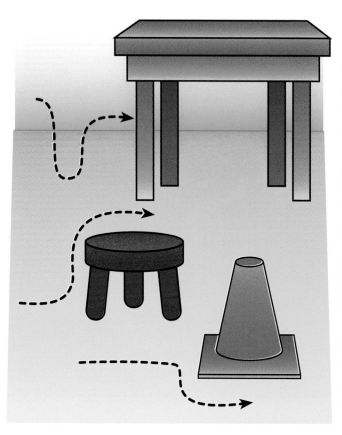

Walk This Way

Over, through, or around? Which way should we walk to avoid this obstacle? Youngsters will ponder these questions as they maneuver themselves through an obstacle course. Take students to a playground area with assorted equipment or to a prearranged obstacle course. Ask the children to maneuver through the course from a predetermined start to finish point, deciding how to handle each obstacle as they approach it. Take photos of the children as they move under, through, over, and around objects in the course. Use the photos to create a class book titled "Our Walk." As a follow-up activity, read *Rosie's Walk* by Pat Hutchins (Macmillan Publishing Company); then guide youngsters in a discussion of the ways in which Rosie avoided obstacles during her walk.

Kristin Bates—Gr. K, Turner Elementary
West Chicago, IL

Mystery Story

Invite youngsters to use their powers of reasoning to solve this literary mystery. Cover a children's book with a plain book cover. Over a brief period of time—perhaps a week—read the book to your class several times, without revealing the illustrations in the book. At the end of the designated period, remove the cover from the book; then place the book on a shelf in your reading center. Inform students that the mystery book has been shelved for them to discover. After several students have identified the book, read it again to the class, this time showing the pictures and text. Youngsters will delight in the challenge of finding the mystery book— and will discover many other reading delights along the way!

Lynn Cagney—Gr. K, Hunter's Green Elementary
Tampa, FL

Adventurous Astronauts

Encourage your little ones to create their own outer-space adventures with this activity. Enlarge the astronaut pattern on page 153; then duplicate the pattern on white construction paper for each child. Help each child cut out his pattern and the helmet shield of his astronaut cutout; then invite him to embellish the pattern as he desires. Glue a photo of each child behind the cut-out area of his astronaut pattern so that his face shows through the opening. Encourage each child to tell about an imaginary space adventure while you write his dictation on a sheet of paper. Attach each child's astronaut and story to a construction-paper spacecraft cutout; then attach the spacecrafts to a bulletin board titled "Adventurous Astronauts" to create an out-of-this world display.

Sandra O'Connell—Gr. K, M. M. Pierce Elementary
Remington, VA

I blasted off to the moon. I saw a zillion stars on my way. I took some with me in my pocket!

Bagged And Bound

Bag up some pages to make interesting class-created books based on popular children's books. To begin, read aloud a children's book of your choice. Then give each child a 5" x 6" tagboard card. Assign each child a separate page of the book to illustrate on his card; then write his dictated statement about his picture on the card. Put each child's card into a separate zippered plastic sandwich bag and seal the bag tightly. Sequence the bagged pages; then bind the zippered sides of the bags between two tagboard covers. Write a title for the book on the front cover. Read the published book to youngsters again; then read the class version of that book. Place both books in the reading center for youngsters to share and compare. Student interest in books is bound to be in the bag with this idea!

Kay Dawson—Gr. K, B. C. Charles Elementary
Newport News, VA

The Very Happy Hippo

He showed his big teeth in a big smile.

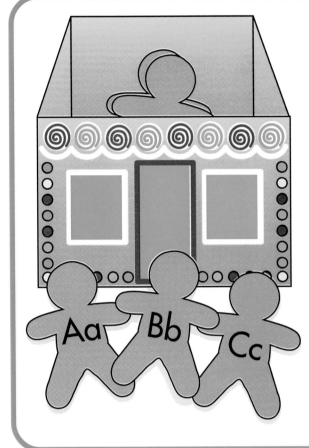

Gingerbread War

Reinforce letter sequencing with a gingered version of the card game known as "War." To make the cards, cut out 26 gingerbread-man shapes from brown paper bags. Label each cutout with a different letter of the alphabet; then laminate the cutouts for durability. Place the stacked cutouts—or cards—facedown in a box decorated to resemble a gingerbread house. To play, have each child in a group of two to four players draw a card from the stack. Ask the players to keep their cards facedown until they receive a signal to turn them over. At that time, encourage the youngsters to determine which of the revealed letters comes first in the alphabet. The child with that letter card keeps all the cards in that round. Continue play in the same manner until all the cards have been revealed. This challenging game will keep youngsters alert and gingerly reviewing the letters of the alphabet.

Jackie Wright—Gr. K And Preschool
Summerhill Children's House, Enid, OK

Larger-Than-Life Letters

Involve youngsters in creating an impressive alphabet display. As you introduce each letter of the alphabet, provide the class with a large bulletin-board paper cutout of that letter. Have the students collectively decorate the cutout with one or more items that begin with that letter—such as confetti, cotton, or crayons for *C.* Display the completed letters on a spacious wall with lots of room to add each newly created letter. At the end of the school year, invite each child to select one of the letters to take home as a keepsake of this larger-than-life alphabet.

Nancy Tatum—Gr. K
D. J. Montague Elementary
Williamsburg, VA

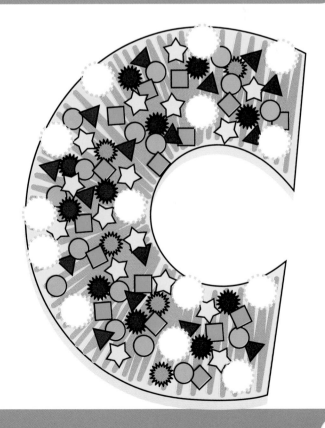

Signs, Signs, Everywhere Are Signs

Hand signs, that is! Expose youngsters to a different form of communication with hand signing. Post an alphabet hand-sign chart in a prominent place in your classroom. Explain to students that some people use hand signs to communicate in addition to, or instead of, speaking. Then teach youngsters how to sign the alphabet. To further encourage their use of signing, invite children to sign the letters in their names, their initials, color names, and basic vocabulary. Add books with hand signs to your reading center, and enhance the reading of familiar books with hand signs. To prompt youngsters to use signs in dramatic play, provide a doll with a hearing aid attached to one of its ears (the aid can be sewn on or attached with a piece of Velcro®). Soon your class will be seeing signs all around.

Glenda Singer—Pre-K, The Country School
North Hollywood, CA

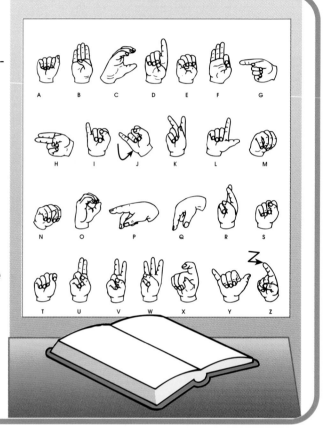

Skill Sandwiches

Hungering for new ways to practice rhyming skills? Then invite your students to build rhyming sandwiches. To prepare, duplicate the desired number of sets of sandwich patterns on page 158 on construction paper, being sure to make two copies of the bread slice for each set. Cut out each of the patterns; then program each set with a different rhyming word set—such as *cat, fat, bat, sat,* and *hat.* Laminate the cutouts for durability. Then place all the pieces in a basket. To use, have a child select a bread slice from the basket, then find and stack each of the corresponding sandwich fixings to create a rhyming sandwich. Encourage him to continue in this same fashion until he has assembled sandwiches from all the pieces in the basket. Mmmm! Rhyming sandwiches—just the thing to satisfy those hungry appetites!

Karen Eiben—Preschool, The Kids' Place, LaSalle, IL

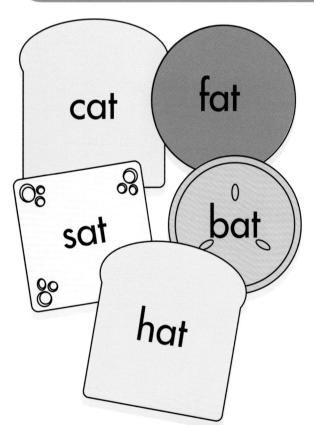

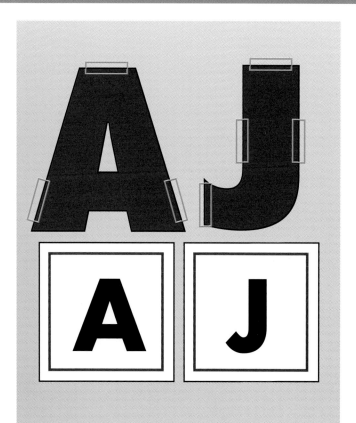

Letter Lineup

Here's a lineup procedure loaded with learning opportunities! Laminate a set of construction-paper letter cutouts to represent the entire alphabet. Tape the cutouts on the floor in random order to form a line. Program a separate notecard for each letter. When you are ready for youngsters to line up, give each child a letter card; then ask him to stand on the corresponding floor letter. After students are able to identify letters, simply tell each child which letter to stand on. Later in the year, challenge each youngster to stand on the letter which begins a named word—such as "boy" or "pan." You'll be delighted to have a letter-perfect line every time!

Amber Peters—Gr. K
Parkview A+ Cultural Arts Magnet
High Point, NC

Jolly Jump-Up

Youngsters will do some jolly jumping when you initiate this game as a time filler or a magnet to draw students together for group activities. Program each of 26 notecards with a different letter of the alphabet. Then program six additional cards with a jumping stick figure and "Jolly Jump-Up!" Shuffle the cards; then keep them in an accessible place. Whenever your class has a few unscheduled minutes, or you want to call the attention of youngsters to form a group, simply grab the stack of cards and hold it up so that students can see the bottom card. If the card reveals a letter, the students call out that letter name. If the card reveals the jumping figure, youngsters jump up and call out "Jolly Jump-Up!" Continue flashing cards until students have gathered or time is up. What a jolly good jumping time!

Jill Coolbroth—Gr. K
Meadow Lake Elementary
New Hope, MN

Out-Of-Sight Alphabet

With this activity, students may make the letters disappear from their sights, but not from their memories! Write each letter of the alphabet on a chalkboard or dry-erase board. Invite each student, in turn, to find a named letter on the board, then erase that letter. Later in the year, you might write both uppercase and lowercase letters on the board and have students locate and erase the specified letter. Or have each youngster erase the letter with which a given word begins. No matter how you choose to challenge youngsters with this activity, they will have an out-of-sight, into-the-mind experience!

Susan Schneider—Gr. K
Durham Elementary
Durham, NY

"Alpha-Basket"

This basket of goodies is full of initial letter learning opportunities. Decorate a large basket; then label it with the letter that your class is currently studying. Ask each student to look around the classroom to find an item that begins with that letter; then have him place the item in the basket. Challenge youngsters to bring from home an item or picture that begins with that letter. When the child brings his item to school, label it with his name; then have him put the item in the basket. Periodically remove the items from the basket and review the initial sound of the letter under study. A-tisket, a-tasket, there's learning in the basket!

Sharon W. Caniglia—Three- And Four-Year-Olds
First Baptist Preschool And Kindergarten Of St. Charles
Waldorf, MD

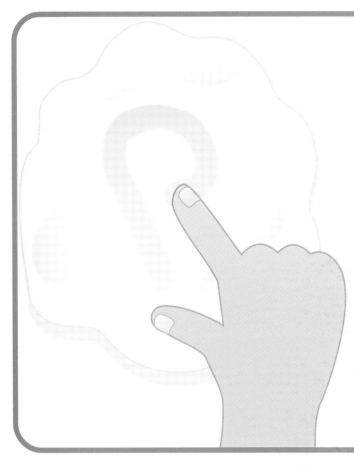

Letters À La Lather

Lather up a sensational writing experience with this neat suggestion. After reviewing each letter of the alphabet, invite students to practice writing the letter in shaving cream. For each child, simply spray a small mound of shaving cream onto a clean tabletop or a laminated construction-paper mat programmed at the top with the letter being studied. Encourage each child to spread the cream, then use his finger to form the letter in the cream. Have him "erase" his letter by smoothing over the lather; then encourage him to write the letter again. Continue the activity as student interest dictates. To clean up, have youngsters wipe the table, then wash the lather off their hands. Letter writing is so easy! Just lather, letter, and repeat.

Beth Wineberger—Gr. K
P. S. 116Q-William C. Hughley
Jamaica, NY

Alphabet Annual

Create a class yearbook that will have alphabetical appeal to youngsters throughout the year and in years to come. Label each page in a photo album with a different letter of the alphabet. Take a photograph of each child in your class; then arrange the photos in the album according to the first letter of each child's name. Also include photos of significant adults in the school. Invite youngsters to find, or to illustrate, a picture of a real or imaginary person to display on the pages to which no photos correspond. Keep the annual updated by adding photos of new students. Use the album to reinforce initial letter sounds and associations. At the end of the year, you might donate the annual to the school library—and be pleasantly surprised at how many of your former students check it out! This is one annual activity worth repeating each year.

Susanna Walz—Gr. K, Center School, Easthampton, MA

Wonderful "Alpha-Worm"

Use a student-created "alpha-worm" to help teach the letters of the alphabet as well as to provide an interesting classroom display. To make the "alpha-worm," have youngsters help you paint 27 paper plates with an assortment of watercolor paints. Then assign each child a letter. Encourage the child to find and cut out a magazine picture of something that begins with that letter. Or ask him to draw a picture that corresponds to his letter. Then have the child glue the picture and a die-cut, construction-paper letter onto a painted plate. Draw an appealing face on the extra paper plate. Then display the letter plates in sequence with the face mounted at the beginning of the alphabet. Youngsters will delight in referring to their "alpha-worm" time and again as they become alphabet-wise throughout the year.

Eva Excaliber—Three- And Four-Year-Olds, Play and Learn Preschool
Miami, FL

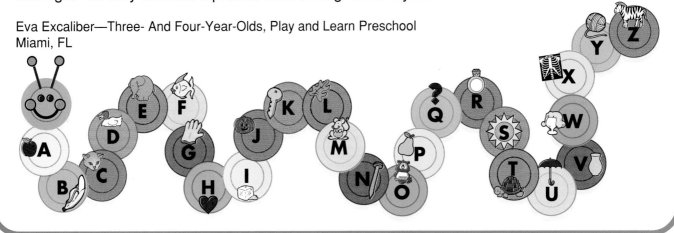

Letter Lessons

Reinforce your lessons on each letter of the alphabet with some of these tips. In advance, ask youngsters to bring in a picture—such as a magazine cutout or photo—that begins with the letter being studied. When each student brings his picture to class, write a word card for the picture, then discuss its initial sound with the class. Attach each of the pictures and the corresponding word cards to a bulletin-board display labeled with a large uppercase and lowercase cutout of that letter. Encourage youngsters to use the display pictures and words as they engage in writing activities. Replace the letter cutouts, pictures, and word cards with items corresponding to the next letter to be studied. Place the removed pictures and word cards in a class book titled "Letter Lessons." Invite youngsters to take turns taking home the book to share with their parents. After every letter is represented in the book, add it to your class library as a reading and writing reference book for students.

Margaret Smith—Gr. K, St. Augustine, Troy, NY

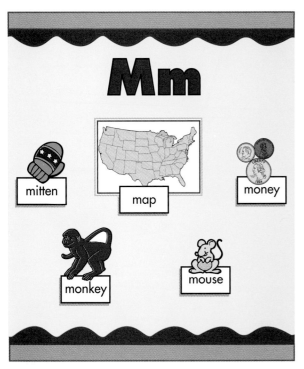

Shopping A To Z

Invite youngsters to use their shopping savvy in this alphabet shopping game. In advance, program each of 26 paper grocery bags with a different letter of the alphabet. Give each child a bag to take home. Ask her to find a food or kitchen item that begins with the letter sound on her assigned bag, then return the item in her bag. After all the bags and items have been returned, display all the items in a mock store; then set out the bags in alphabetical order. Invite each child to take a turn selecting an item from the store and putting it into the appropriate bag. Continue the shopping spree until every item has been placed in its corresponding bag. After playing several rounds, put the bags and items in a learning center so youngsters can shop 'til they drop. Or at least until they run out of alphabet items!

Kimberly Rizzo—Gr. K
Together We Grow Childhood Center
Lake Havasu, AZ

Wall Of Words

Build the vocabulary of your youngsters with a word wall. To make a wall, purchase a plain shower curtain; then use colored vinyl tape to create a large grid on the curtain so that it resembles a brick wall. Hang the curtain on a wall or so that it can be used as a room divider. As you introduce new individual or rhyming family words to your students, program a separate card—or brick—with each word. Use the word bricks to reinforce word recognition skills; then attach each brick to a box on the word wall. Encourage youngsters to refer to the word bricks during their reading and creative-writing activities. Keep the word wall on display throughout the school year, adding to it brick by brick; then watch the wall grow as you watch youngsters build rock-solid vocabulary and writing skills.

Seema Gersten
Harkham Hillel Hebrew Academy
Beverly Hills, CA

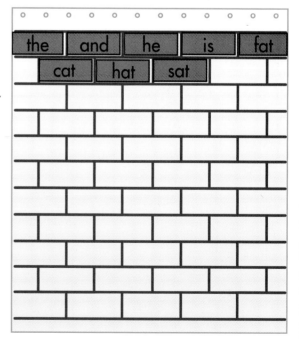

The Wonders Of Watermelon

Explore a watermelon with your youngsters. Bring in a whole melon and discuss its size, shape, and color. Encourage the students to look around the room and name items with an attribute like the melon. Cut a slice of watermelon for each child. Give him a spoon or a craft stick. For a little fine-motor practice, ask him to remove the seeds from his slice and set them aside to dry. As he is working, talk about the texture of the fleshy part of the watermelon. Make a list of describing words that volunteers come up with. Challenge the child to count the number of seeds he found in his slice. Compare the number to another child's find. Is it more or less? Continue this critical thinking until interest wanes; then invite the children to eat the evidence. Juicy, juicy, juicy!

Joyce Bank—Three- And Four-Year-Olds
Jewish Community Center
Margate, NJ

juicy
red
squishy
runny
soft
mushy

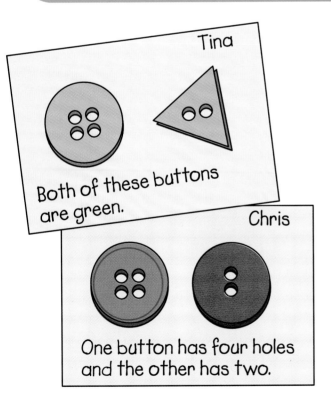

Tina

Both of these buttons are green.

Chris

One button has four holes and the other has two.

Button Bonanza

Invite small groups of children to look through a collection of buttons. Allow for a time of free exploration with the buttons. (Supervise youngsters closely as buttons can be a choking hazard.) Challenge each group to collectively sort the buttons by a particular attribute. Have each child find two buttons that are alike. On an index card write the child's dictation describing how they are alike; then tape or glue the buttons to the card. Then ask her to find two buttons that are different and repeat the activity. Divide a bulletin board in half. Label one half "Alike" and the other half "Different." Post the cards showing the discoveries under the correct headings.

Tracy Tavernese—Pre-K
Holy Child School
Old Westbury, NY

Let Me See That!

Place magnifying glasses near the classroom pet for better observation. Your youngsters will enjoy seeing little paws holding food, little teeth nibbling, tiny eyes blinking, or tiny fins moving in the water. They will be fascinated by this up close and personal view.

Diane Shatto—Three- And Four-Year-Olds
St. Elizabeth
Kansas City, MO

Glorious Gunk

Have you ever played with gunk? Now's your chance! For each pair of children, pour 1/2 cup of liquid starch and 1/2 cup of glue into a quart-size resealable bag. Seal the bag and encourage the two children to mix the ingredients by squishing and squashing the bottom of the bag with their hands. (Be sure they keep the bag upright.) If desired, add food coloring once the items are well-mixed. Allow the children to take their gunk out of the bag and feel its texture. After some free exploration, work on concepts with your students. Can they make the gunk long, short, thick, thin, etc.? A great sensory workout for those little fingers, this gunk is no junk!

Christy Coleman—Three- And Four-Year-Olds
Lakeside YMCA
Metairie, LA

Just Chillin'

Add ice cubes to the water table along with scoops and scales for some cool discoveries. Youngsters are sure to experience the properties of water as well as explore the differences in temperature. For added fun, mix food coloring with the cubes, in two primary hues, before freezing. As the ice melts in the water, a secondary color will appear. Isn't that cool? Your little ones will think so!

Jennifer Peña—Pre-K
Normandy Village
Jacksonville, FL

Magical Metamorphosis

Conclude a butterfly unit with this life-cycle project. Each child will need a 6" x 30" strip of foamboard, two sheets of green construction paper, a large dried bean, a plastic lei, a wooden stick, black yarn, a craft stick, two pipe cleaners, a sheet of white construction paper, and colored squares of tissue paper.

To prepare, make wing patterns from tagboard (to fit on the white paper), pour some diluted glue into cups, and gather a supply of paintbrushes and hole punchers. Assist your youngsters in completing the following steps to make each stage of the butterfly's life cycle. Me, oh my, what a great butterfly!

Egg: Cut a leaf shape from a sheet of green paper. Glue the leaf to the left end of the foamboard strip. Glue the bean (egg) onto the leaf.

Caterpillar: Cut a leaf shape from a sheet of green paper. Use hole punchers to take "bites" out of the leaf. Glue the leaf to the strip as shown. Twist the ends of the plastic lei; then staple the ends and center of the lei (caterpillar) to both the leaf and board. Shape a pipe cleaner to resemble antennae; then staple it in place.

Chrysalis: Wrap a length of black yarn around the end of a stick. (Or if there is a twig sprouting from the stick, wrap the yarn around the twig so that the chrysalis looks as though it's hanging.) Secure the yarn's end with glue; then glue or tape the stick to the board next to the caterpillar.

Butterfly: Trace the wing patterns onto the white paper and cut them out. Decorate the wings by attaching colored tissue-paper squares with a paintbrush and diluted glue. To make the butterfly's body, wrap a length of black yarn around the craft stick and secure the yarn's end with glue. Bend a pipe cleaner in half and insert it under the wrapped yarn for antennae. Glue the butterfly body and wings to the right end of the foamboard strip as shown.

Kari Murray—Gr. K
Lincoln School
West Allis, WI

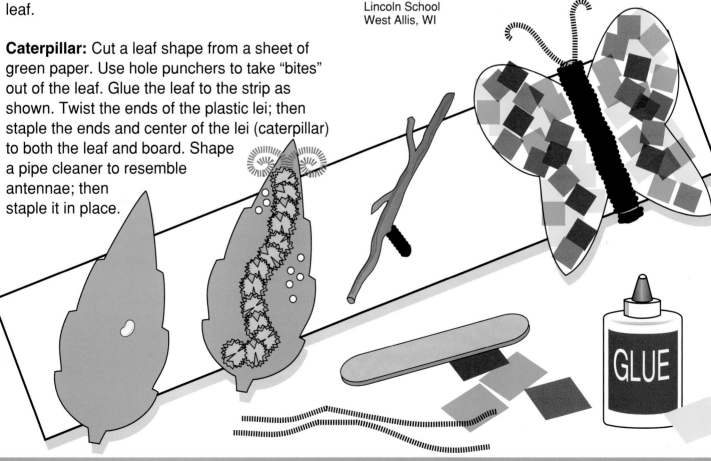

Fingerpainting Fun

Put some feeling into your next fingerpainting activity. Divide the fingerpaint into four containers. Mix a different substance into each container—such as salt, sand, rice, small pasta, or cornmeal. When distributing the paint, put a small glob from each mixture in each corner of the child's paper instead of just one big glob in the middle. Be ready for lots of exciting descriptions and discoveries during this extrasensory experience!

Thai Cole—Special Education
Highland Park Learning Center Magnet School
Roanoke, VA

What's In A Nest?

Lots of interesting discoveries will be made when youngsters examine the composition of a bird's nest. Place the nest on top of a covered table. Provide tweezers, magnifying glasses, and rubber gloves for children to use. Make a list of the building materials as they are discovered. Make sure hands are washed and the tabletop is sanitized after cleanup. Those bird builders are incredible!

Jane Hall—Four-Year-Olds
Trinity Church Day School
Long Green, MD

Poking Around In Potpourri

Set up a wonderful discovery center by emptying a bag of potpourri onto a tray and providing magnifying glasses and rubber gloves (for those who may have allergies). Challenge the children to name and sort the many different items that make up the sweet smelling mixture. Your little ones are sure to become potpourri professionals and may start mixing up their own concoctions on the playground!

Karen Eiben—Preschool
The Kids' Place
LaSalle, IL

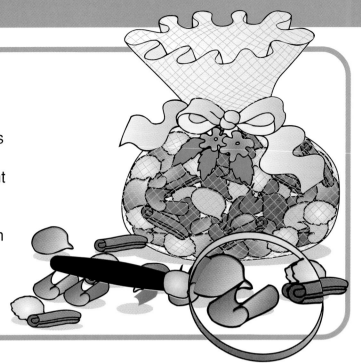

Bring The Zoo To You

Is a field trip to the zoo not possible? Here's a fun way to improvise! Invite your students to bring stuffed animals from home. Learn the basics about each animal—how it moves, what it eats, where it lives, and how it sounds. Show real photos of the animal if possible. Once all the animals are discussed, see how many different ways they can be sorted. End the sorting practice by categorizing the animals according to their habitats. Divide the children into the same number of groups as there are habitats. Give each group a piece of bulletin-board paper and ask them to paint or color a background for one of the animal habitats.

To conclude this animal unit, invite youngsters to come to class the following day dressed and ready for a field trip—with sunglasses, binoculars, bag lunch, hats, etc. Before they arrive, set up the chairs in your room to resemble bus seating. Hang the backdrops outside on a nearby wall or fence with the stuffed animals grazing below. As youngsters come in, have them take a seat on the bus. "Drive" the children to the zoo singing animal songs as you travel. When you arrive at the zoo, walk to each habitat exhibit and ask volunteers for information about the animals found there. Finish the trip with a picnic lunch while an animal-sounds recording plays in the background. What a great learning experience, and you never left the school grounds!

Cindy Ashcraft—Preschool Hearing Impaired
Mesa Schools
Chandler, AZ

Rainmaker

Extend a weather unit by making rain for your little ones. You will need a glass jar with a lid, hot water, and ice cubes. Fill the jar half full with hot water. Attach the lid and put the jar in a warm spot. Place the ice cubes on top of the jar. Have children observe the jar for a few minutes. What did they discover? It's raining, it's pouring...

Alison Hovda—Gr. K
St. Patrick's School
Fayetteville, NC

Pop, Pop! Fizz, Fizz!

Youngsters will delight in watching these magical popcorn kernels dance! Fill a glass with water. Add ten popcorn kernels. Drop in two Alka-Seltzer® tablets (or a generic brand of the same type of medicine). Have children watch to see what happens. The kernels will start going up and down. It's magic! No, not really. There's a complex scientific reason concerning air, gas, and buoyancy. If you want to explain the reasoning, simplify it by saying that the bubbles attach to the kernel and make it float to the top in the same way a swim ring full of air helps a child float. Once the bubbles reach the top of the water, they pop. That makes the kernel heavy again so it sinks back down. If no explanation is necessary, simply let the children marvel in the discovery.

Alison Hovda—Gr. K

Bottled Tornado

Put a spin on your weather unit with this terrific twister. Fill a flat-bottomed plastic bottle three-fourths full with water. Add a drop of food coloring and a drop of dish detergent to the water. Drop a marble in the bottle; then screw the lid on tightly.

To make a "tornado" appear, invert the bottle and swirl it around in a circular motion. Stop swirling the bottle. Watch for a tiny vortex that will be spinning in the water. Your little ones will be fascinated with this bottle! Take this opportunity to discuss with them the dangers of tornadoes and emergency procedures to follow if tornadoes are possible in your area.

Alison Hovda—Gr. K

Look At My Shadow!

Prove to your little ones that the earth is spinning by recording the lengths of their shadows during the day. Pair up your students one sunny morning. Provide each pair with a piece of chalk. Take them outside to a paved location. Have one child from each pair stand in a line, side by side, facing the same direction. Instruct each of the other children to use the chalk to trace the footprints of his partner. Assist each child with writing his partner's name next to the prints. Then have each child mark a line on the pavement at the top of his partner's shadow. Have the partners change jobs and do the same activity on another spot of pavement. Ask for predictions of what might happen when this activity is done later in the day. Return to the location at midday. Ask each child to stand on his marked footprints as his partner marks the top of his shadow. What happened? Ask for predictions again and return at the end of the day for one more recording. Your little ones will love having fun with the sun!

Diane Parette—Gr. K
Durham Elementary
Durham, NY

Bubbles Below Freezing

Turn a frightfully cold day into Bubble Day to explore the concept of freezing. Mix up a batch of bubble solution using the recipe shown. Gather a supply of various bubble wands, from coat hangers to pipe cleaners. Bundle up your class and head outdoors. Invite the children to blow and blow and blow. They will soon discover that these bubbles don't always pop. Some will freeze and bounce! What a fun way to be introduced to the properties of water.

Gelatin Bubbles

1 quart of water
1/2 cup of gelatin
1/8 cup of glycerin
2 teaspoons of Dawn® dishwashing detergent

Heat the water and add gelatin. Stir until the gelatin is dissolved. Add glycerin and detergent. Mix well.

Kelly Crook—Gr. K
Blue Hill Elementary
Blue Hill, NE

Crickets In The Classroom

Strengthen a unit on insects by setting up a cricket habitat for observation. Crickets can be purchased at local pet stores (as food for other animals) or from Carolina Biological Supply (1-800-334-5551). Keep these insects in a small lidded aquarium. Provide cardboard egg cups for the crickets to use as homes. Place a cotton ball moistened with water in a jar lid and put it in the aquarium for the crickets to drink. Youngsters will enjoy feeding the crickets dry dog food or small pieces of fruit. For an up close and personal look, place one of the crickets in a small plastic bottle or bug viewer. The crickets won't be the only ones chirping in the room!

Tricia Draper—Gr. K
Millarville Community School
Turner Valley, Alberta

They're Here!

After 21 days of waiting, we are proud to announce the arrival of Tweety, Markus, and Ferdinand. They broke into this world on Monday, March 4, 1996, at 12:05 P.M.

Their weights:
Tweety: 9 cubes
Markus: 11 cubes
Ferdinand: 8 cubes

Please come by and welcome our new arrivals!

Hear Ye, Hear Ye!

If you and your students are hatching chicks in an incubator, be sure to issue these cute announcements when the big day arrives! Prepare a blank announcement similar to the one shown. Have your youngsters agree on a name for each chick. Record the time of birth on the chalkboard. Have your students help you weigh each chick with a nonstandard unit of measurement, such as linking cubes or teddy bear counters. Fill in the announcement with the correct information; then duplicate a copy for each child. Encourage students to share their announcements with someone at school or their parents. Science, math, and language skills will be hatching in your classroom! Peep, peep!

Shana L. Brock—Gr. K
Wendell Watson Elementary
Lakeland, FL

Counting Jar

A counting jar full of thematic manipulatives will entice your students to count, sort, and pattern! Find a quart-size plastic jar with a lid. Use a paint pen to write "Counting Jar" on the side of the jar; then use paint pens and stickers to decorate the jar. Each week, fill the jar with manipulatives that relate to your theme, such as attribute blocks for a shape theme or acorns and chestnuts for an autumn theme. Also provide a duplicated class list near the jar. Encourage youngsters to sort and pattern with the manipulatives in the jar during free time. Ask each child to count the items in the jar and record his answer next to his name on the class list. At the end of the week, invite youngsters to help you count the items in the jar and check the accuracy of their answers. Then replace the manipulatives to match your next theme and keep interest high.

Becky Krapf—Gr. K
Richard Mann Elementary
Walworth, NY

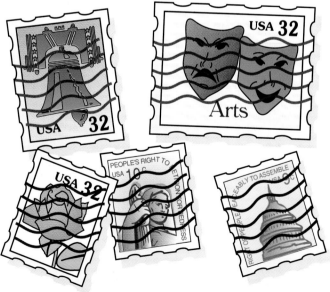

Stamp Collection

Save cancelled stamps from your mail to use as interesting math manipulatives. Simply snip the stamped corners off envelopes or, better yet—ask families to save stamps for you. When you have enough stamps, invite youngsters to use them for counting, sorting, patterning, numeral recognition, or number sequencing. Free and easy!

Cathy Armstrong—Gr. K
Bain Elementary School
Charlotte, NC

I Know Numbers!

Try this fun review of the numbers 1–10. For each child, divide a large sheet of construction paper into ten sections—labeled 1–10—allowing more space for larger numbers. For each child, prepare a set of numeral cutouts (1–10) and corresponding sets of small objects to glue onto each section of the paper.

Ask each child to find the appropriate numeral cutout to glue over each numeral on his paper. Then instruct him to count specific objects to glue on each section; for example, *one* pom-pom, *two* sea-shells, *three* sequins, etc. Invite little ones to take their projects home so they can proudly show off their number knowledge.

Leslie H. Wagner—Three-, Four-,
   And Five-Year-Olds
Immanuel Christian Preschool
Powell, WY

Drink-Cup Surprise

Take advantage of every part of the school day to slip in a little learning! Before snacktime or lunch, use a permanent marker to write a numeral or draw a shape on the outside bottom of each child's clear, plastic drink cup. Then watch children's faces light up when they discover this surprise! Mark the cups on a regular basis, and math matters will become the talk of the table.

Jennifer Englund—Three-, Four-, And Five-Year-Olds, Cambridge Manor Day Care, Fairfield, CT

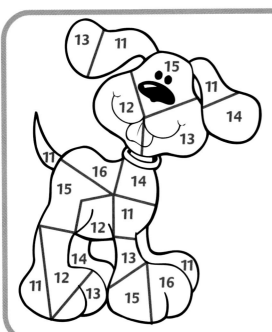

Find The Numbers

A search-and-find game will provide fun practice with recognizing teen numbers. On a small sheet of poster board, draw a simple outline of an animal or object. Divide the outline into sections and write a teen number in each section. Laminate the drawing for repeated use. Then label a blank die with corresponding teen numbers. Provide a wipe-off marker or crayon. Have a youngster roll the die, find all the teen numbers on the drawing that match the number on the die, and shade those labeled sections. Have her continue until the entire drawing is shaded. Then have her wipe off the drawing for the next child to use. For extra practice, reduce the drawing, make copies, and send this activity home.

Kyle Welby—Gr. K, Epstein Hebrew Academy, St. Louis, MO

Head For The Border!

If you're looking for pictures for patterning practice, take a look at your bulletin-board borders. Find a border with a built-in pattern. Leave part of a strip intact; then cut apart the repeated pictures on the remaining section. Now youngsters can use the individual pictures to match the strip, extend the pattern shown on the strip, or create new and different patterns of their own!

Catherine Wyshyvanuk—Gr. K
St. Francis Xavier
Phoenix, AZ

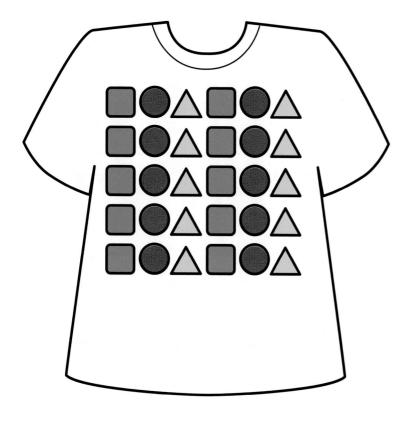

Paint A Pattern

Conclude a unit on patterning by making these pattern-painted T-shirts. Request that each child bring a solid, light-colored T-shirt from home. Provide various colors of fabric paint and sponges cut into basic shapes.

Working with one or two children at a time, lay each shirt flat on a tabletop. Slip a thin piece of cardboard or a section of newspaper inside each shirt (to prevent paint bleeding through). Then invite each youngster to work from top to bottom and left to right as he paints the pattern of his choice onto his shirt. Check the directions on the fabric-paint bottle to set the paint, if necessary, and allow the paint to dry at least overnight. Then invite youngsters to wear their pattern shirts with pride!

Christy Cochran—Gr. K
Dallas Elementary, Dallas, GA

Family Graph

Use a subject that youngsters know well—their own families—as the basis for a simple graph. List your students' names down the left side of a long length of bulletin-board paper. Then duplicate enough copies of the people patterns on page 159 so that each child has at least one set and there are several extras. Ask each youngster to cut out patterns that correspond to the members of her family (matching the males, females, adults, and children). Help each child write each family member's name on a corresponding pattern. Then help each child glue her family patterns to the prepared graph, in a row next to her name.

When everyone has added her family patterns to the graph, have youngsters count the number of people in each child's family. Help youngsters make comparisons. Who has the *most* family members? Who has the *fewest?* Which children have *equal* numbers of people in their families?

Tracy Tavernese—Four-Year-Olds
Holy Child School
Old Westbury, NY

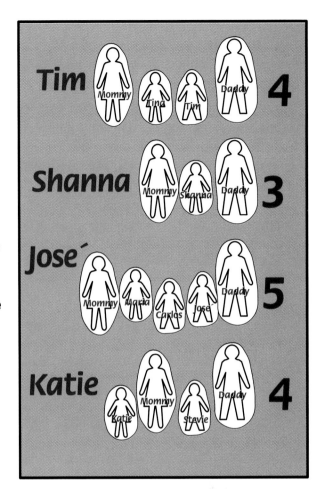

Candy Classification

There's no trick to getting youngsters interested in sorting and graphing—just use Halloween treats! Invite each child to sort his Halloween candy and other goodies. (Use treats from a class party or have children bring in their treats from home.) Have youngsters separate their treats into categories such as candy bars, gum, toys, stickers, lollipops, etc. After a child has sorted his goodies into groups, have him line up his treats to make a simple graph. Encourage each child to count and compare the number of treats in each category.

Carmen Rufa—Gr. K
Samaritan Children's Center, Troy, NY

Count The Votes

Elect to take a vote when you need to make a whole-group decision. Draw a visual reminder of the choices on your chalkboard; then attach an envelope below each choice. Distribute a blank slip of paper to each child. Ask each student to place his slip in the envelope below his choice. Then empty the envelopes one at a time and count together to see which choice got the most votes. Majority rules!

Darlene V. Martino—Four- And Five-Year-Olds
Palmyra Head Start
Palmyra, NY

What shape shall we make our jack-o-lantern's eyes?

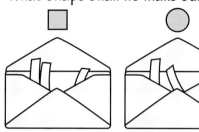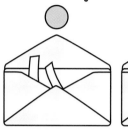

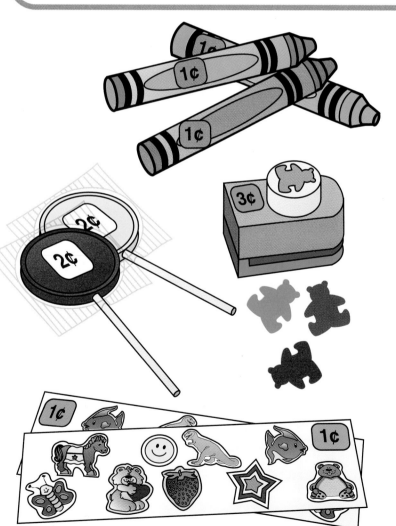

Shopping Day

Plan a Shopping Day to give little ones practice with counting. To prepare, ask parents to donate small, inexpensive items—such as stickers, lollipops, or tiny toys from fast-food restaurants. Have each child bring in 10 pennies. Enlist the help of parent volunteers or older children to serve as clerks for each department of the classroom store. Price the items between one and five cents. Before the spree begins, have each child decorate a paper lunch bag to serve as a shopping bag.

When all is ready, invite each child to look over the merchandise and count out pennies for each purchase. Youngsters will even experience the need to "budget" when their penny supplies get low.

Debbie Quigley—Parent Education
Sweetwater Adult School
National City, CA

Counting Cookies

Cookies made with M&M's® have math practice baked right into them! Before beginning to bake, read *The M&M's® Counting Book* by Barbara Barbieri McGrath (Charlesbridge Publishing). Then bring out a bag of M&M's® and invite youngsters to sort them into color groups. Mix up a batch of cookies following your favorite sugar-cookie recipe or the one on the back of the M&M's® bag. Encourage student volunteers to count out specific numbers of M&M's® to add to the batter. For example, ask a child to add four red M&M's® and three yellow M&M's®. Continue until all the candies are added; then bake and cool the cookies as directed by the recipe. When it's time to eat, have each youngster count how many of each color of candy he finds in his cookie.

Sharon W. Caniglia—Three- And Four-Year-Olds
First Baptist Preschool and Kindergarten of St. Charles
Waldorf, MD

100

90	91	92	93	94	95	96	97	98	99
80	81	82	83	84	85	86	87	88	89
70	71	72	73	74	75	76	77	78	79
60	61	62	63	64	65	66	67	68	69
50	51	52	53	54	55	56	57	58	59
40	41	42	43	44	45	46	47	48	49
30	31	32	33	34	35	36	37	38	39
20	21	22	23	24	25	26	27	28	29
10	11	12	13	14	15	16	17	18	19
0	1	2	3	4	5	6	7	8	9

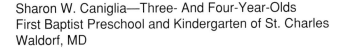

Mouse Count

This versatile hundreds chart will get daily use in your classroom! Print the numbers 0–99 on sentence strips, ten numbers per strip, as shown. Print all the numbers divisible by ten in red and all the numbers ending in five in blue. Print the number 100 in red on a separate strip. Back the strips with colored construction paper and laminate them for durability. Arrange the strips in order in a pocket chart. Then make a felt mouse and hot-glue it to a clothespin. Each day, invite a student volunteer to move the mouse to the next number on the chart. When you reach the number 100, have a classroom celebration! You can also use the chart to count down the days until the end of the school year.

Use the number strips to help youngsters practice counting by ones, fives, and tens and to practice numerical order, too.

Barbie Bauman—Gr. K
Pasadena Fundamental School
St. Petersburg, FL

Numbers In Sequence

Sequencing numbers is as easy as 1-2-3 with this display idea. Decorate a bulletin board to fit your current theme. Locate reproducible patterns to match the theme. Have each child color and cut out a copy of a reproducible. Then label each cutout with a numeral in a sequence—such as 1–20 or 10–30. Display the children's cutouts in random order on the board.

Each day, invite a volunteer to choose a cutout. Remove this cutout from the board and display it in front of your group. Then ask volunteers to find the cutouts labeled with the next few numerals in sequence. Replace the cutouts and start with a different numeral the next day.

Sandra O'Connell—Gr. K
M. M. Pierce, Remington, VA

Pearls And Shells

This numeral/set matching game is especially suited to a study of the ocean. Collect several large, flat shells. Use a permanent marker to write a numeral on the inside of each shell. Place the shells in your water table (or a fish tank) and add some blue food coloring to the water. Place a bucket of white marbles or pearl beads nearby. To use the center, have each youngster fish a shell out of the water, identify the numeral printed on it, and place a corresponding number of pearls into the shell.

Patricia McIntyre—Gr. K
Beechwood On The Bay
Quincy, MA

Tootsie Roll® Match

Little ones will love this sweet game! Use the Tootsie Roll® pattern on page 159 to cut ten Tootsie Roll® shapes from black paper. Use a white paint pen or correction pen to write "Tootsie Roll®" on one side of each cutout. Then cut each roll into two pieces. Write a numeral between one and ten on one piece and attach the corresponding number of star stickers onto the other piece. Laminate all the pieces for durability. For added fun, store the pieces in a Tootsie Roll® bank. Then encourage youngsters to match the numerals to the corresponding sets.

Laurie Mills—Gr. K, Stevenson Elementary,
Stevenson, AL

Haunted House Counting

For some ghoulishly good math practice, invite each child to construct a haunted house. In advance create a supply of lima-bean ghosts. Simply use a permanent marker to draw a ghost face on one side of each small, dried bean. Then duplicate the house pattern on page 160 two times for each child—once on orange construction paper and once on black construction paper. Ask each child to cut out the two patterns. Assist each child in cutting four windows and a door in the black pattern (as shown). Then have each child open the flaps and glue the black house atop the orange one.

Invite younger children to glue any number of ghosts in each open space. Encourage them to count the ghosts in each window and doorway. For more advanced learners, use a piece of chalk to label the windows and doors of each house with numerals 1–5. Ask students to glue the corresponding number of bean ghosts in each open space.

Wendy Castriotta—Three-And Four-Year-Olds
St. Leo's School
Leominster, MA

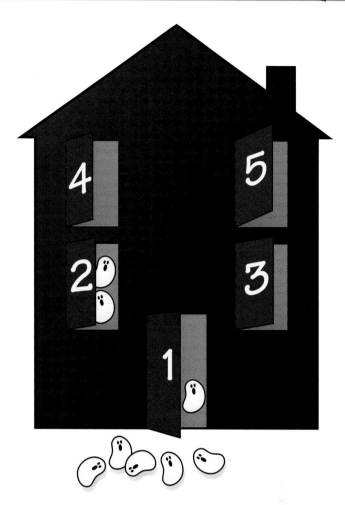

Beans In The Box

This independent activity will help students practice numeral recognition, sets, and fine-motor skills. Purchase an embroidery-floss storage box from your local craft store. At the bottom of each small compartment, glue a slip of paper with a numeral printed on it. Store a supply of dried beans and a pair of tweezers in the larger compartment on the side of the box. To do the activity, a child opens the box, identifies each numeral, and uses the tweezers to place the corresponding number of beans into each compartment.

Amy Pierce—Pre-K
Pierce Private Day School
Irving, TX

Number Hoops

Little ones can practice simple equations with the help of their friends and a few Hula-Hoops®. Place five hoops on the gym floor or an open grassy space. Leave one hoop empty. Have one child stand in the second hoop, two children in the third hoop, three in the fourth hoop, and four in the fifth hoop. Then have each remaining child take a turn rolling a die. He identifies the number on the die, then surveys the hoops to see where he can stand in order to make a corresponding set. For example, if he rolls a one, he can stand in the empty hoop, which will then show a set of one. If he rolls a five, he can join the hoop with four children to make a set of five. (He'll need to take a friend along if he rolls a six!) Continue play until all the hoops are filled. Then start over with new children in the hoops.

Mark Pittelkow—Four-Year-Olds
Merrick Community Services Preschool
St. Paul, MN

Daily Lunch Equations

If you take a lunch count each morning, don't miss out on important opportunities for math practice. Divide your class into groups, or use tables or work groups you've already assigned. Ask one child in each group to be in charge of counting and recording (with symbols, tally marks, or numerals) the number of children in her group who brought their lunches from home and the number who need school lunches.

Once each group's totals are established, print the equation on the chalkboard for the whole class to see. Talk students through the addition process as you determine the lunch count for the entire class. After they've mastered this activity, provide new challenges by writing the equation vertically, writing it out as a story problem, or even illustrating the totals on a graph. So much to learn from a simple lunch count!

Shana L. Brock—Gr. K and 1
Wendell Watson Elementary
Lakeland, FL

School

Our Daily Lunch Equation:
School Lunches:
Blue Table: ___1___
Green Table: ___5___
Yellow Table: ___0___
Red Table: ___2___
Total: ___8___

5			
4			
3			
2			
1			
	Blue	Green	Yellow	Red

Home

Our Daily Lunch Equation:
Home Lunches:
Blue Table: ___3___
Green Table: ___1___
Yellow Table: ___4___
Red Table: ___5___
Total: ___13___

5			
4			
3			
2			
1			
	Blue	Green	Yellow	Red

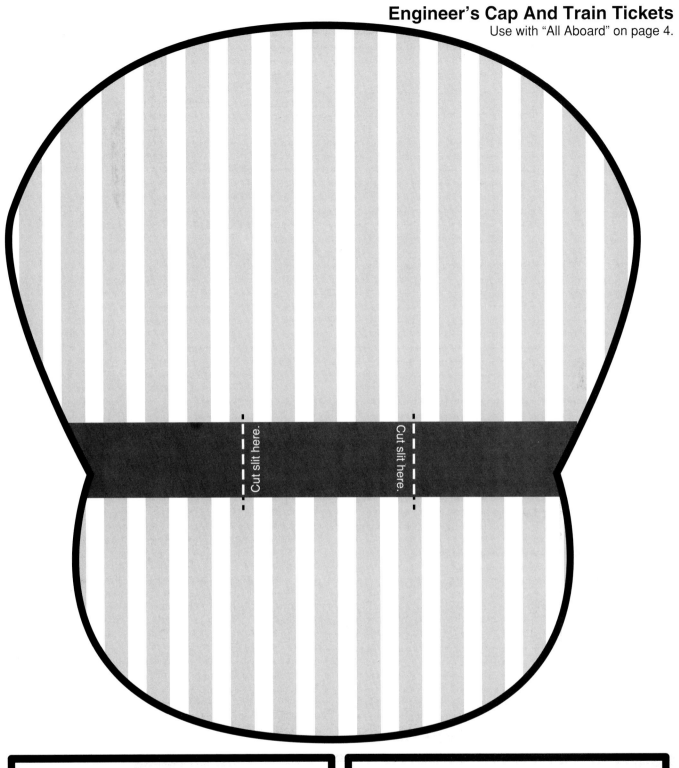

Cut slit here.

Cut slit here.

CLASSROOM TICKET
All Aboard For
A Great Year!
ADMIT ONE

CLASSROOM TICKET
All Aboard For
A Great Year!
ADMIT ONE

Apple Pattern
Use with "Eye-Appealing Apple Name Cards" on page 5.

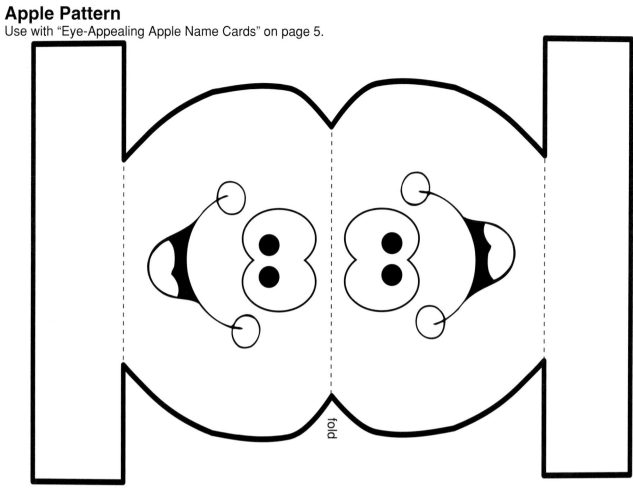

fold

Pumpkin Pattern
Use with "Perky Pumpkins" on page 13.

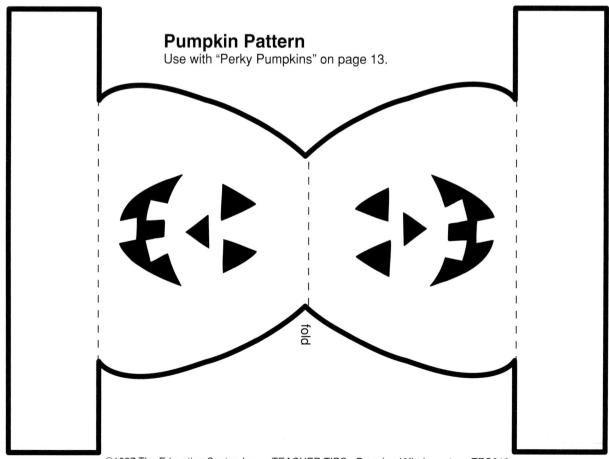

fold

Camera Pattern

Use with "Picture-Perfect Behavior" on page 42 and "Picture Yourself In..." on page 68.

Progress Report Form

Use with "Rootin'-Tootin' Progress Reports" on page 57.

A
Cheer For

_____

Rah! Rah! Rah!
Sis boom bah!
See what I know!
Rah! Rah! Rah!

Color: _____
Shape: _____
Letter(s): _____
Number(s): _____
Other: _____

©1997 The Education Center, Inc. • TEC810

Squirrel Patterns

Use with "Going Nuts Over Good Behavior" on page 42 and "Scampering Squirrels" on page 116.

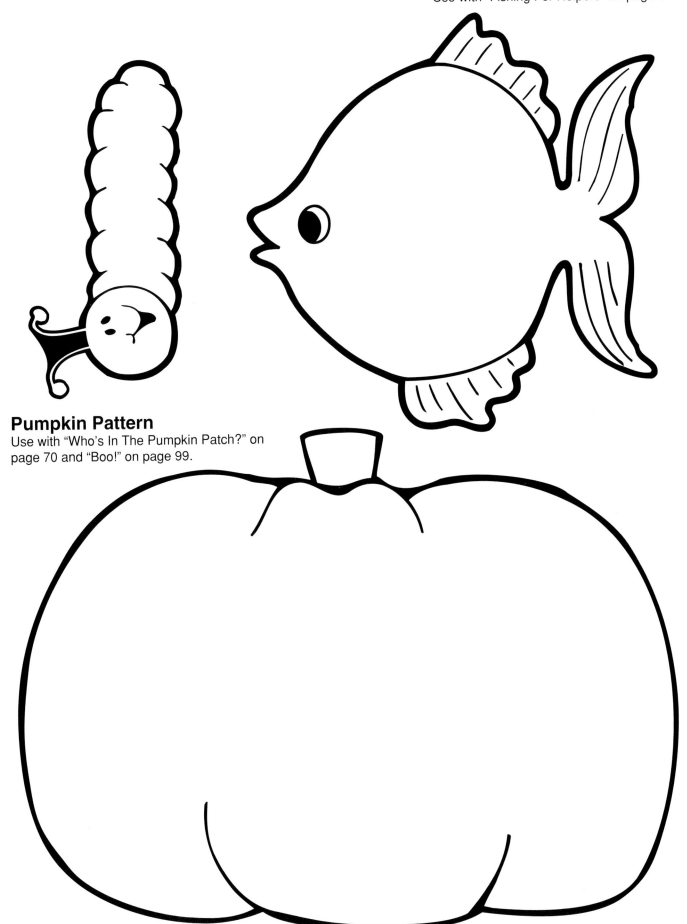

Worm & Fish Patterns
Use with "Fishing For Helpers" on page 64.

Pumpkin Pattern
Use with "Who's In The Pumpkin Patch?" on page 70 and "Boo!" on page 99.

Plane And Pilot Pattern
Use with "Welcome To Our Community" on page 66.

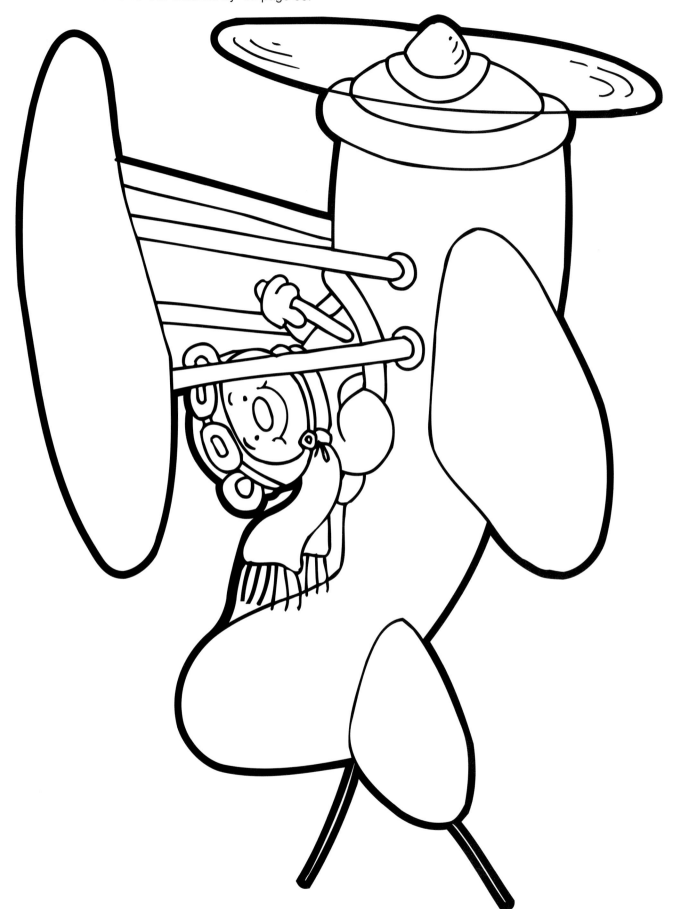

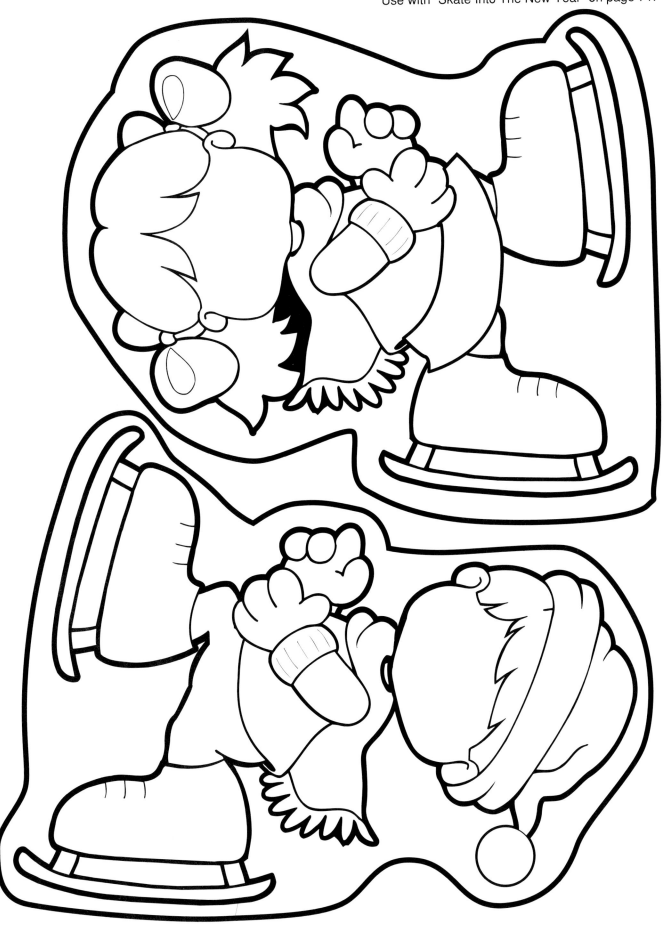

Reading Chick Patterns

Use with "Crack Open A Good Book" on page 72.

fold

fold

©1997 The Education Center, Inc. • *TEACHER TIPS* • *Preschool/Kindergarten* • TEC810